I0021231

Building ETL Pipelines with Python

Create and deploy enterprise-ready ETL pipelines by employing modern methods

Brij Kishore Pandey

Emily Ro Schoof

BIRMINGHAM—MUMBAI

Building ETL Pipelines with Python

Copyright © 2023 Packt Publishing

Group Product Manager: Reshma Raman

Publishing Product Managers: Birjees Patel and Heramb Bhavsar

Content Development Editor: Shreya Moharir

Project Coordinator: Hemangi Lotlikar

Technical Editor: Rahul Limbachiya

Copy Editor: Safis Editing

Proofreader: Safis Editing

Indexer: Subalakshmi Govindhan

Production Designer: Prashant Ghare

DevRel Marketing Coordinator: Nivedita Singh

First published: September 2023

Production reference: 1250923

Published by Packt Publishing Ltd.

Grosvenor House

11 St Paul's Square

Birmingham

B3 1RB

ISBN 978-1-80461-525-6

www.packtpub.com

To my daughter, Yashvi, who lights up my life; to Khushboo, my wife, my rock, and my inspiration; to my parents, Madhwa Nand and Veena, who taught me everything I know; and to my brothers, who have always stood by my side.

– Brij Kishore Pandey

Contributors

About the authors

Brij Kishore Pandey stands as a testament to dedication, innovation, and mastery in the vast domains of software engineering, data engineering, machine learning, and architectural design. His illustrious career, spanning over 14 years, has seen him wear multiple hats, transitioning seamlessly between roles and consistently pushing the boundaries of technological advancement.

Hailing from the renowned SRM Institute of Science and Technology in Chennai, India, Brij's academic foundation in electrical and electronics engineering has served as the bedrock upon which he built his dynamic career. He has had the privilege of collaborating with industry behemoths such as JP Morgan Chase, American Express, 3M Company, Alaska Airlines, and Cigna Healthcare, contributing immensely with his diverse skill set. Presently, Brij assumes a dual role, guiding teams as a principal software engineer and providing visionary architectural solutions at ADP (Automatic Data Processing Inc.).

A fervent believer in continuous learning and sharing knowledge, Brij has graced various international platforms as a speaker, sharing insights, experiences, and best practices with budding engineers and seasoned professionals alike. His influence doesn't end there; he has also taken on mentorship roles, guiding the next generation of tech aficionados, in association with Mentor Cruise Inc.

Beyond the world of code, algorithms, and systems, Brij finds profound solace in spiritual pursuits. He devotes times to the ardent practice of meditation and myriad yoga disciplines, echoing his belief in a holistic approach to well-being. Deep spiritual guidance from his revered guru, Avdhoot Shivanand, has been pivotal in shaping his inner journey and perspective.

Originally from India, Brij Kishore Pandey resides in Parsippany, New Jersey, USA, with his wife and daughter.

Emily Ro Schoof is a dedicated data specialist with a global perspective, showcasing her expertise as a data scientist and data engineer on both national and international platforms. Drawing from a background rooted in healthcare and experimental design, she brings a unique perspective of expertise to her data analytic roles. Emily's multifaceted career ranges from working with UNICEF to design automated forecasting algorithms to identify conflict anomalies using near real-time media monitoring to serving as a subject matter expert for General Assembly's Data Engineering course content and design. Her mission is to empower individuals to leverage data for positive impact. Emily holds the strong belief that providing easy access to resources that merge theory and real-world applications is the essential first step in this process.

About the reviewers

Adonis Castillo Cordero has been working in software engineering, data engineering, and business intelligence for the last five years. He is passionate about systems engineering, data, and leadership. His recent focus areas include cloud-native landscape, business strategy, and data engineering and analytics. Based in Alajuela, Costa Rica, Adonis currently works as a lead data engineer and has worked for Fortune 500 companies such as Experian and 3M.

I'm grateful for my family and friends' unwavering support during this project. Thanks to the publisher for their professionalism and guidance. I sincerely hope the book brings joy and is useful to readers.

Dr. Bipul Kumar is an AI consultant who brings over seven years of experience in deep learning and machine learning to the table. His journey in AI has encompassed various domains, including conversational AI, computer vision, and speech recognition. Bipul has had the privilege to work on impactful projects, including contributing to developing software as a medical device as the head of AI at Kaliber Labs. He also served as an AI consultant at AIX, specializing in developing conversational AI. His academic pursuits led him to earn a PhD from IIM Ranchi and a B.Tech from SRMIST. With a passion for research and innovation, Bipul has authored numerous publications and contributed to a patent application, humbly making his mark on the AI landscape.

Table of Contents

Part 1: Introduction to ETL, Data Pipelines, and Design Principles

1

2

3

Design Principles for Creating Scalable and Resilient Pipelines   31

Part 2: Designing ETL Pipelines with Python

4

Sourcing Insightful Data and Data Extraction Strategies   43

5

Data Cleansing and Transformation   53

6

Loading Transformed Data   71

7

Tutorial – Building an End-to-End ETL Pipeline in Python   81

8

Powerful ETL Libraries and Tools in Python   93

Part 3: Creating ETL Pipelines in AWS

9

A Primer on AWS Tools for ETL Processes   117

10

Tutorial – Creating an ETL Pipeline in AWS   129

11

Building Robust Deployment Pipelines in AWS   143

Part 4: Automating and Scaling ETL Pipelines

12

Orchestration and Scaling in ETL Pipelines   155

13

Testing Strategies for ETL Pipelines   169

14

Best Practices for ETL Pipelines   185

15

Use Cases and Further Reading 197

Index 209

Other Books You May Enjoy 220

Preface

We're living in an era where the volume of generated data is rapidly outgrowing its practicality in its unprocessed state. In order to gain valuable insights from this data, it needs to be transformed into digestible pieces of information. There is no shortage of quick and easy ways to accomplish this using numerous licensed tools on the market to create "plug-and-play" data ingestion environments. However, the data requirements of industry-level projects often exceed the capabilities of existing tools and technologies. This is because the processing capacity needed to handle large amounts of data increases exponentially, and the cost of processing also increases exponentially. As a result, it can be prohibitively expensive to process the data requirements of industry-level projects using traditional methods.

This growing demand for highly customizable data processing at a reasonable price point goes hand in hand with a growing demand for skilled data engineers. Data engineers handle the extraction, transformation, and loading of data, which is commonly referred to as the **Extract**, **Transform**, **and Load** (**ETL**) process. ETL workflows, also known as ETL pipelines, enable data engineers to create customized solutions that are not only strategic but also enable developers to create flexible deployment environments that can scale up or down depending on any data requirement fluctuations that occur between pipeline runs.

Popular programming languages, such as SQL, Python, R, and Spark, are some of the most popular languages used to develop custom data solutions. Python, in particular, has emerged as a frontrunner. This is mainly because of its adaptability and how user-friendly it is, making collaboration easier for developers. In simpler terms, think of Python as the "universal tool" in the data world – it's flexible and people love working with it.

Building ETL Pipelines in Python introduces the fundamentals of data pipelines using open source tools and technologies in Python. It provides a comprehensive guide to creating robust, scalable ETL pipelines broken down into clear and repeatable steps. Our goal for this book is to provide readers with a resource that combines knowledge and practical application to encourage the pursuit of a career in data.

Our aim with this book is to offer you a comprehensive guide as you explore the diverse tools and technologies Python provides to create customized data pipelines. By the time you finish reading, you will have first-hand experience developing robust, scalable, and resilient pipelines using Python. These pipelines can seamlessly transition into a production environment, often without needing further adjustments.

We are excited to embark on this learning journey with you, sharing insights and expertise that can empower you to transform the way you approach data pipeline development. Let's get to it!

Who this book is for

This book is a comprehensive guide to ETL data pipelines in Python. It is targeted toward data enthusiasts and software professionals who want to learn about the core concepts of ETL designs and applications. To get the most out of this book, a basic understanding of Python is recommended.

What this book covers

Chapter 1, A Primer on Python and the Development Environment, introduces Python, the core of this book. You must have prior experience with Python to understand this book. This chapter will not cover anything in detail; instead, it will give a primer on Python that's needed for this book. Also, it will illustrate how to set up a development environment with an IDE and check out the code in Git.

Chapter 2, Understanding the ETL Process and Data Pipelines, explains the ETL process and the significance of a robust ETL pipeline. This starts with an example of how and when to implement an ETL process and how a good pipeline can help automate the ETL process. This also explains the difference between ETL and ELT.

Chapter 3, Design Principles for Creating Scalable and Resilient Pipelines, deals with the implementation of the best design patterns with open source Python libraries to create an enterprise-grade ETL pipeline. It illustrates how to install these libraries and primers on all the functions available to create robust pipelines. This also explains all the design patterns and approaches available to create an ETL process.

Chapter 4, Sourcing Insightful Data and Data Extraction Strategies, deals with sourcing data from different source systems. Firstly, we identify an open source to get high-quality, insightful data that can act as an input for ETL pipelines. Secondly, we discuss various strategies to ingest the sourced data.

Chapter 5, Data Cleansing and Transformation, deals with various data transformation techniques in Python. We start with a hands-on example of data cleansing and massaging. We also learn how to handle missing data. Finally, we apply various transformation techniques to transform the data in the desired format

Chapter 6, Loading Transformed Data, deals with various data loading techniques in Python. We start with a hands-on example of data loading in an RDBMS and then we repeat this process for NoSQL databases. We'll also learn about various use cases of data loading. Finally, we'll look into some of the best practices for data loading.

Chapter 7, Tutorial – Building an End-to-End ETL Pipeline in Python, creates a full-fledged ETL pipeline using various tools and technologies we have learned about so far. We'll source data, ingest data, transform data, and finally, load the data into final tables. We use the MySQL database for the example.

Chapter 8, Powerful ETL Libraries and Tools in Python, explores various open source tools to create a modern data pipeline. First, we'll explore Python libraries such as Bonobo, Odo, mETL, and Riko. We'll go through the pros and cons and create an ETL pipeline by applying these libraries. Finally, we'll move to big data and study tools such as Apache Airflow, Luigi, and pETL.

Chapter 9, A Primer on AWS Tools for ETL Processes, explains various AWS tools for creating ETL pipelines. It goes from explaining various strategies to selecting the best tools and design patterns. You'll learn how to create a development environment for AWS and deploy the code locally. We'll also explore the best strategies for deployment and testing. Finally, we'll use some automation techniques to automate boring stuff.

Chapter 10, Tutorial – Creating an ETL Pipeline in AWS, creates an ETL pipeline in AWS in conjunction with Python. We start by creating a mini pipeline using a step function and AWS Lambda. Then, we go on to create a full-fledged pipeline using Bonobo, EC2, and RDS.

Chapter 11, Building Robust Deployment Pipelines in AWS, creates a basic CI/CD pipeline for ETL jobs. We'll use AWS CodePipeline, CodeDeploy, and CodeCommit to create a robust CI/CD pipeline to automate the code deployment. We'll see an example of how Git can be leveraged for a CI/CD pipeline in AWS. We'll also get familiar with using Terraform for code deployment.

Chapter 12, Orchestration and Scaling in ETL Pipelines, covers the limitations of ETL pipelines and how to scale ETL pipelines to handle increasing demand seamlessly. It goes on to explain how to choose the best scaling strategies. It also explains how to create robust orchestration for ETL pipelines. Finally, we'll work on a hands-on exercise to create an ETL pipeline and apply scaling and orchestration strategies.

Chapter 13, Testing Strategies for ETL Pipelines, deals with ETL testing strategies. A pipeline may contain bugs and it is very important to catch them before they make it to production. Unit testing using pytest does cover most errors, but an external ETL testing strategy is central to creating a high-performance, resilient ETL pipeline.

Chapter 14, Best Practices for ETL Pipelines, covers some of the industry best practices for creating ETL pipelines in production. It also identifies some of the common pitfalls that users should avoid while building ETL pipelines.

Chapter 15, Use Cases and Further Reading, covers practical exercises and mini-project outlines, with further reading suggestions included in this chapter. Also, it exposes you to a use case of creating a robust ETL pipeline for New York yellow-taxi data for analysis. Finally, we'll get US construction market data through AWS Marketplace and create a production-ready, fault-tolerant, high-quality data pipeline in AWS.

To get the most out of this book

To effectively utilize the resources and code examples referenced within this book, ensure that your system meets the following technical requirements:

Software/hardware covered in the book	Operating system requirements
PyCharm 2023.2	Windows, macOS, or Linux
Jupyter Notebook 7.0.2	
Python 3.6+	

We recommend using PyCharm as the preferred **Integrated Development Environment** (IDE) for working with Python, and we might make specific references to PyCharm throughout this book. However, you are free to use any Python-compatible IDE of your choice.

We also recommend installing `pipenv` as it is used for managing dependencies.

Download the example code files

You can download the example code files for this book from GitHub at https://github.com/PacktPublishing/Building-ETL-Pipelines-with-Python. If there's an update to the code, it will be updated in the GitHub repository. We recommend that you fork and clone the repository to your local machine

We also have other code bundles from our rich catalog of books and videos available at https://github.com/PacktPublishing/. Check them out!

Conventions used

There are a number of text conventions used throughout this book.

`Code in text`: Indicates code words in text, database table names, folder names, filenames, file extensions, pathnames, dummy URLs, user input, and Twitter (now, X) handles. Here is an example: "For example, let's write a simple data pipeline that imports three CSVs, `traffic_crashes.csv`, `traffic_crash_vehicle.csv`, and `traffic_crash_people.csv`, as input data."

A block of code is set as follows:

```
# Merge the three dataframes into a single dataframe
merge_01_df = pd.merge(df, df2, on='CRASH_RECORD_ID')
all_data_df = pd.merge(merge_01_df, df3, on='CRASH_RECORD_ID')
```

When we wish to draw your attention to a particular part of a code block, the relevant lines or items are set in bold:

```
aws lambda create-function  -s3-key-function ReverseStringFunction \
--zip-file fileb:// s3_key_function.zip --handler lambda_function.
lambda_handler \
--runtime python3.8 --role <YOUR IAM ARN ROLE>
```

Any command-line input or output is written as follows:

```
psql -U postgres
```

Bold: Indicates a new term, an important word, or words that you see onscreen. For instance, words in menus or dialog boxes appear in **bold**. Here is an example: "Select **System info** from the **Administration** panel."

> **Tips or important notes**
> Appear like this.

Get in touch

Feedback from our readers is always welcome.

General feedback: If you have questions about any aspect of this book, email us at customercare@packtpub.com and mention the book title in the subject of your message.

Errata: Although we have taken every care to ensure the accuracy of our content, mistakes do happen. If you have found a mistake in this book, we would be grateful if you would report this to us. Please visit www.packtpub.com/support/errata and fill in the form.

Piracy: If you come across any illegal copies of our works in any form on the internet, we would be grateful if you would provide us with the location address or website name. Please contact us at copyright@packtpub.com with a link to the material.

If you are interested in becoming an author: If there is a topic that you have expertise in and you are interested in either writing or contributing to a book, please visit authors.packtpub.com.

Share Your Thoughts

Once you've read *Building ETL Pipelines with Python*, we'd love to hear your thoughts! Scan the QR code below to go straight to the Amazon review page for this book and share your feedback.

https://packt.link/r/1-804-61525-0

Your review is important to us and the tech community and will help us make sure we're delivering excellent quality content.

Download a free PDF copy of this book

Thanks for purchasing this book!

Do you like to read on the go but are unable to carry your print books everywhere?

Is your eBook purchase not compatible with the device of your choice?

Don't worry, now with every Packt book you get a DRM-free PDF version of that book at no cost.

Read anywhere, any place, on any device. Search, copy, and paste code from your favorite technical books directly into your application.

The perks don't stop there, you can get exclusive access to discounts, newsletters, and great free content in your inbox daily

Follow these simple steps to get the benefits:

1. Scan the QR code or visit the link below

https://packt.link/free-ebook/978-1-80461-525-6

2. Submit your proof of purchase
3. That's it! We'll send your free PDF and other benefits to your email directly

Part 1: Introduction to ETL, Data Pipelines, and Design Principles

For the first part of this book, we will introduce the fundamentals of data pipelines in Python and set up your local development environment with **Integrated Development Environments** (IDEs), virtual environments, and Git version control. We will provide you with an overview of what **Extract-Load-Transform** (ETL) data pipelines are and how to design them yourself. As a word of caution, Python is at the core of this book; you must have a basic familiarity with Python in order to follow along accordingly.

This section contains the following chapters:

- *Chapter 1, A Primer on Python and the Development Environment*
- *Chapter 2, Understanding the ETL Process and Data Pipelines*
- *Chapter 3, Design Principles for Creating Scalable and Resilient Pipelines*

A Primer on Python and the Development Environment

Whether your production environment caters to only one data pipeline at a time or a whole multitude of overlapping systems, the core tenets of data environment management remain the same.

We have dedicated this chapter to breaking down the foundational roots of all successful applications by discussing the basic principles of the Python programming language and how utilizing package management applications can create clean, flexible, and reproducible development environments. We will walk you through a step-by-step tutorial on how to install and establish a basic Git-tracked development environment that will prevent future confounding modular incompatibilities from impacting the successful deployment of your data pipelines in production.

By the end of this chapter, you will have a strong understanding of why Python is a powerful tool that can be used to develop highly-customized and powerful data transformation ecosystems. We will cover the following topics:

- Python fundamentals
- Using Python attributes to build an application's foundation
- Key attributes of an effective development environment
- Downloading and installing a local **integrated development environment** (IDE)
- Creating and cloning a Git-tracked repository into your IDE
- Managing project packages and circular dependencies with a **module management system** (MMS)

Introducing Python fundamentals

Since Python is the language in which we will design pipelines, it is a good idea to go through Python's core fundamentals.

Python is a general-purpose, dynamically typed programming language with a highly versatile nature that can be powerfully used for scripting, object-oriented, procedural, or functional programming. Built on top of C, a low-memory but complex imperative procedural language that efficiently maps machine instructions with minimal runtime support, this human-readable language has become one of the most popular programming languages of the 21st century.

Python's ubiquitous nature is echoed by its vast online community and well-supported open source libraries.

In this section, we are going to cover the following topics:

- Python data structures
- `if...else` conditions
- Looping techniques
- Python functions
- Object-oriented programming using Python
- Working with files in Python

To brush up on the key concepts necessary for ETL pipelines, let's take a look at each of these topics in detail so that we can understand them better.

An overview of Python data structures

Here are the data structures available natively in Python:

- **List**: This is like a one-dimensional dynamic array but can hold heterogeneous or homogeneous elements separated by commas. Python lists are mutable and ordered. Like arrays, the index of the first item is 0. The index of the last item in a list starts from -1 and counts arguments toward the beginning in descending order. Lists are represented by []. An index can be used to get a value from a list. In the following section, we will discuss some of the most important indexing operations on lists:

    ```
    sample_list = [1, "another", "list", "a", [3,4]]
    print(sample_list[0]) # 1
    print(sample_list[1]) # "another",
    print(sample_list[-1]) # [3,4]]
    print(sample_list[1:4])# ["another", "list", "a"]
    print(sample_list[:4])# [1, "another", "list", "a"]
    print(sample_list[3:])# ["a",[3,4]]
    ```

    We can work with lists in Python using a variety of methods that are available for working with lists.

Python list methods can be found in the following documentation: `https://docs.python.org/3/tutorial/datastructures.html`.

- **Dictionary**: Dictionaries are like HashMaps in Python. Dictionaries are represented by key-value comma-separated pairs inside curly braces. Dictionary keys are unique and can be of any Python immutable data type except for a few. The main purpose of a dictionary is to store a value with some key and return the value for that key when needed. Like lists, there are various methods for dictionaries:

```python
sample_dict = {"Key1": "Value1", 2: 3, "Age": 23}
print(sample_dict["Age"]) # 23
print(sample_dict[2]) # 3
```

  You can refer to the following documentation for more details on dictionary methods: `https://docs.python.org/3/tutorial/datastructures.html#dictionaries`.

- **Tuple**: Tuples are an ordered collection of elements. Like lists, they can hold both heterogeneous and homogenous data. The only major difference between a tuple and a list is that tuples are immutable while lists aren't.

  Tuples are represented by parentheses or round brackets:

```python
sample_tuple = (1,"2","brij")
print(sample_tuple [0]) # 1
```

  Refer to the following documentation for more details on tuples: `https://docs.python.org/3/tutorial/datastructures.html#tuples-and-sequences`.

- **Sets**: Python sets are collections of items that are unordered, changeable, and do not allow duplicate values. It is useful to use sets when you need to store a collection of elements, but do not care about order or duplicates.

  Like dictionaries, sets are represented by curly braces:

```python
sample_set = {5,9}
sample_set.add(4)
print(sample_set) # {5,9,4}
sample_set.remove(9)
print(sample_set) # {5, 4}
```

In this section, we covered Python data structures. Other data structures, such as the frozen set, are not very frequently used, so we will skip them.

In the next section, we will discuss if...else conditions in Python.

Python if...else conditions or conditional statements

We often need decision-making capabilities in programming languages to execute a block of code based on certain conditions. These are known as if...else conditions or conditional statements.

A conditional statement in Python allows you to specify a certain action to be taken only if a certain condition is met. This is useful because it allows you to make your code more efficient by only performing certain actions when they are necessary.

For example, if you wanted to check if a number is divisible by 3, you could use a conditional statement to only perform the division operation if the number is actually divisible by 3. This would save time and resources because you would not have to perform unnecessary calculations.

The following is an example of a sample if...else condition:

```
'''In this program,
we check if a number is divisible by 3 and
display an appropriate message'''


num = 9
# Try below two as well:
# num = 7
# num = 6

if num  == 0:
    print("This is a Zero")
elif num%3 ==0:
    print("Number is divisible by 3")
else:
    print("Number is not divisible by 3")
```

Those of you who are familiar with Python will be aware that the else-if condition in Python is symbolized by elif. The next section will be dedicated to looping techniques, so let's get started!

Python looping techniques

A loop iterates over a sequence or block of code until a condition is met or until a fixed number of iterations are performed.

The Python language supports various looping techniques. They are very useful in programming and in maintaining code structures. Unlike traditional loops, they also save time and memory by avoiding the need to declare extra variables. There are two types of loops in Python:

- **for loop**: Python for loops are used to traverse through sequences such as strings, lists, sets, and so on. Once started, the loop continues until it reaches the last element of the sequence. The break statements terminate the iteration prematurely:

```
    # Program to return a list of even number from a given list
  # Given list
  numbers = [7,4,3,5,8,9,8,6,14]
```

```
# Declare an empty list
even_numbers = []# iterate over the list
for num in numbers:
    #Add the even numbers to even_numbers list
    if num%2 == 0:
     even_numbers.append(num)print("The Even number list is ",
numbers)
```

- **while loop**: `while` loops in Python are used to iterate through sequences until a given condition is satisfied. The `while` loop will continue indefinitely if a condition is not given:

```
count = 0
while (count < 11):
    print ('The current number is :', count)
    count = count + 1
print('While loop terminates here.')
```

Now that we have gained an understanding of Python loops, let's move on to discussing functions. Functions are a vital part of Python programming as they allow us to create reusable blocks of code that can be easily executed multiple times. By utilizing functions, we can write more efficient and organized code, making it easier to debug and maintain. In the upcoming section, we will discuss how to create and utilize functions in our programs.

Python functions

A **function** is a reusable block of code that can be used to execute certain tasks. A Python function starts with the `def` keyword. The Python function can be thought of as a recipe in a cookbook – it tells the computer what steps to follow to complete a certain task. You can give a function a name, and then use that name to call the function whenever you need to perform that task. Functions can also accept input (**arguments**) and can return a result (**return values**). Functions are useful because they allow you to reuse code, making your programs more efficient and easier to read.

The following is an example of a function in Python:

```
def div_of_numbers(num1, num2):
    """This function returns the division of num1 by num2"""
    # This function takes two parameters namely num1 and num2.
    if num2==0:
    #Below is a return statement.
    return 'num2 is zero.'
    else:
    #Below is another return statement.
    return num1/num2
#This is how a python function is called.
```

```
print(div_of_numbers(8,0))
print(div_of_numbers(8,4))
```

We just saw how to write a sample function in Python and call it with arguments. The next step will be to see how a function can be used as a method within a Python class.

Object-oriented programming with Python

Python is a programming language that allows the use of multiple programming paradigms, including object-oriented programming. In object-oriented programming, everything is considered an object, which can have attributes and behaviors. This means that in Python, every element in the language is considered an object. Additionally, Python supports the concept of multiple inheritance, which allows an object to inherit characteristics and behaviors from multiple parent objects. This allows greater flexibility and customization within the language. Overall, Python's support for object-oriented programming and multiple inheritance make it a powerful and versatile language. Let's take a look at this in more detail:

- **Class**: A class is the blueprint of objects. Python uses the `Class` keyword to create a class:

    ```
    Class DataPipeline():
        first_tool = "AirFlow"
    ```

    The following is how we can create an instance (or object) of this class:

    ```
    datapipeline = DataPipeline()
    ```

    We can pass parameters while creating an instance of the class. These parameters are collected in an initializer method known as `__init__`. This method is called as soon as the object is created.

    We can also write functions inside a class. A function inside a class is known as a method.

    A method can be called using a dot operator on the instance of the class. The first parameter is `self`. We can use any names other than `self` but it is discouraged as it will impair the readability of the code.

- **Inheritance**: Inheritance is a fundamental aspect of object-oriented programming that allows developers to create new classes based on the properties and behaviors of existing classes.

    By utilizing inheritance, we can create a new class that inherits the data and methods of an existing class without having to modify the original class in any way. This means that we can create a new class that has all the same features as the original class but with the added ability to modify or extend the inherited data and methods to fit the needs of the new class. Inheritance is a powerful tool that enables developers to create complex and reusable code, and it is a key aspect of object-oriented programming languages such as Java, C++, and Python.

    The following example illustrates inheritance:

    ```
    # parent class
    class DataPipelineBook:
    ```

```
    def __init__(self):
        print("This book is very hot in market")
        self.pages =300

    def what_is_this(self):
        print("Book")

    def pages(self):
        return self.pages
```

The preceding code defines a class called `DataPipelineBook` in Python. A class is a template for creating objects, and an object is an instance of a class.

The `__init__` method is a special method in Python classes that is called when an object is created from a class. It is commonly known as the constructor. In this case, the `__init__` method prints a message to the console and sets the value of the `pages` attribute to 300.

The `what_is_this` method is a regular method that is defined within the class. It simply prints the `Book` string to the console.

The `pages` method is also defined within the class. It returns the value of the `pages` attribute, which is set to 300 in the `__init__` method.

To use this class, you would need to create an object from it and then call its methods. The next step is to create a child class. An example of creating a `child` class is shown here:

```
# child class
class PythonDataPipelineBook(DataPipelineBook):

    def __init__(self):
        # call super() function
        super().__init__()
        print("Create Data Pipeline with Python")

    def what_technology_is_used(self):
        return "Python"

pipeline = PythonDataPipelineBook()
pipeline.what_is_this()
peggy.what_technology_is_used()
```

The preceding code is defining a child class called `PythonDataPipelineBook` that inherits from a parent class called `DataPipelineBook`. The child class has a constructor method (init) that calls the `super()` function to initialize the parent class. It also has a method called what_technology_is_used that returns the `Python` string.

The code then creates an object of the `PythonDataPipelineBook` class called `pipeline` and calls the `what_is_this` method from the parent class on it. Finally, it calls the `what_technology_is_used` method on the `pipeline` object.

Next, we'll talk about how Python handles files.

Working with files in Python

The Python language is powerful and makes handling files a breeze. In Python, several operations can be performed on files, including opening, reading, writing, and appending. Let's take a look at how each of these operations can be performed in Python:

- **Open**: To read or write to a file, you first need to open it. Here's how you can open a file in Python:

  ```
  f = open("yellowtaxidata.txt")
  ```

- **Read, write, or append**: When you open a file, you can specify the mode in which you want to open it. The three most common modes are r (for reading), w (for writing), and a (for appending

  Here's an example of how you can open a file in each of these modes:

  ```
  f = open("test_file.txt", "r")  #This file is opened in read
  mode.
  f = open("test_file.txt", "w") #This file is opened in read
  mode.
  f = open("test_file.txt", "a") #This file is opened in append
  mode.
  ```

- **Close**: Did you know that every time you open a file, it's important to close it once you're finished with it? It's easy to do – just use the `f.close()` function.

  But there's an even better way to ensure your files are closed properly: using a context manager. When you open a file using a context manager, the file is automatically closed once you're done with it. This helps prevent any potential issues or errors that could arise from leaving a file open.

  So, the next time you're working with files, remember to close them properly by using either `f.close()` or a context manager. It's a simple step that can save you a lot of headaches in the long run!

Are you tired of constantly forgetting to close your file after writing to it? Don't worry – Python has a solution for that! Using a context manager, you can easily make sure that your file is closed after performing a write operation.

Take a look at the following code:

```
with open("test_file.txt", "w") as f:
f.write("This is test data")
```

By using the `with` keyword, you can ensure that the `test_file.txt` file will be closed automatically after the write operation is completed. No more worrying about leaving your file open and causing issues down the line!

For more information on file handling in Python, check out the official Python documentation.

In this section, we introduced Python and its various capabilities as a programming language. We saw that Python can be used for scripting, object-oriented programming, functional programming, and creating machine learning models and interactive data visualizations. We also discussed that Python has a large online community and many well-supported open source libraries. We also covered several fundamental Python concepts, including data structures (lists and dictionaries), if-else conditions, looping techniques, functions, object-oriented programming, and working with files.

In the next section, we will learn how to set up a development environment for Python, which will allow us to easily start working with the language. This includes installing the necessary software and tools and configuring our system to support Python development.

Establishing a development environment

Before you hit the ground running creating an exciting project with Python, it is essential to create a development environment with a strong foundation in system integrity.

A unique way to think of a Python project is to think in terms of a lab experiment. When designing a lab experiment, a scientist first starts by jotting down the purpose of the experiment and all possible expected outcomes of the experiment. *Why are we creating this experiment?* and *What outputs do we reasonably expect to get from this experiment?* This frame of reference is important to maintain because it leads into the next, and arguably the most important, perspective: *How can we limit confounding factors from impacting the results?* This is where the idea of a clean, sterile, experimental environment comes to the forefront; this idea is synonymous with the needs of a programming environment with a clear and reproducible workflow.

So, how do we design a development environment that not only limits both known and unknown confounding factors from impacting end-pipeline products but is also highly reproducible and shareable? In this section, we will review the primary building blocks of a highly effective and "sterile" development environment:

- Version control with Git tracking
- Making development easy with local **integrated development environments** (IDEs)
- Documenting environment dependencies with `requirements.txt`
- Utilizing **module management systems** (MMSs)

Let's get started!

Version control with Git tracking

The first step of any programming project is to instantiate a version control repository unique to your environment. This keeps the project's development and production environments in separate buckets.

Several version control systems use the Git version control software and protocol. They each offer similar functionality, but some key differences may make one a better fit for your needs than the others.

We will be using GitHub to track and store our data pipelines throughout this book.

One reason to choose GitHub is that it is the most popular platform for hosting and collaborating on Git repositories. It has a large user base, which means that it is well-supported and has a wealth of resources and documentation available. GitHub also has several features specifically designed for collaboration, such as pull requests, which allow users to propose changes to a repository and discuss them with other contributors before merging them into the main code base.

While there are several internet-hosting Git-tracking providers (GitLab and Bitbucket come to mind), we will be using GitHub to track and store our data pipelines throughout this book.

The importance of Git-tracking your code

You might have seen the term "Git" an uncountable number of times but as a general overview, "Git" is any distributed **version control system** (**VCS**) designed to track changes in source code and manage a code base. GitHub is one of these systems. When you've created and cloned a new GitHub repository onto your local device, any changes you make can be tracked, committed, and pushed up to your online storage location.

It's best practice to get into the habit of always committing and pushing your changes frequently so that your work is backed up with Git; this way, you won't lose all of your hard-earned code if you ever do something silly such as spill coffee all over your laptop... (like we have... more than once...). Additionally, your GitHub repositories serve as a portfolio to showcase your code projects publicly (or keep them private, if you prefer).

GitHub also allows others to contribute to your code base. Git version control enables collaboration without the fear of losing or overwriting changes since multiple developers can work on different branches, and changes can be reviewed and merged through pull requests. Code reviews ensure that the code quality of your projects remains high, and helps catch bugs or issues early in the development life cycle.

Additionally, GitHub can be integrated with various services, such as project management tools and various CI/CD tools, and allows automated testing and deployment of your code. We will learn more about project testing and CI/CD tools later in this book.

For now, we encourage you to leverage Git-tracking with GitHub to push code changes "early and often" so that your work is not only backed up online but you can also add your developing data engineering skills to a public code portfolio.

Before moving on to the next section, take a moment to fork the GitHub repository associated with this book so that it is available in your own personal GitHub profile: `https://github.com/PacktPublishing/Building-ETL-Pipelines-with-Python`.

Making development easy with IDEs

As Python programmers, you most likely have a preference in terms of local development environments. However, to avoid the risk of instilling any redundancies, we will walk you through our preferred local development landscape in case you want to mimic the same workflow we'll follow for this tutorial.

iTerm2

We pride ourselves on being superfans of *strategic laziness*, where we set up programming landscapes that are not only easy on the eyes but also take little to nothing to maintain. As Mac programmers, the Terminal interface can be quite dull; that's why we recommend installing iTerm2, which works well on Macs that run macOS 10.14 or newer. As stated on their website, "*iTerm2 brings the Terminal into the modern age with features you never knew you always wanted.*" Take some time to install and customize your new iTerm2 Terminal so that it's aesthetically pleasing; it's much easier to fall into the creativity of development design when your eyes are intrigued by your Terminal.

You can follow the instructions mentioned here to download and set up iTerm2: `https://iterm2.com/downloads.html`.

PyCharm

Next, we recommend using your newly remodeled Terminal to download our favorite IDE: PyCharm. For those of you unfamiliar with IDEs, you can think of an IDE in a similar fashion to iTerm: a visual interface that not only creates an aesthetically pleasing coding environment but also allows you to quickly, efficiently format and structure files with a few short commands. Our local PyCharm environment will be where we choose to clone the Git repository that we created in the previous section.

You can follow the instructions mentioned here to download and set up PyCharm: `https://www.jetbrains.com/pycharm/download/#section=mac`.

You will also need to register your GitHub account to your new PyCharm app by following these steps: `https://www.jetbrains.com/help/pycharm/github.html`.

Jupyter Notebook

Lastly, since we will be working with data, visualizing sections of DataFrames can be quite difficult in a standard Python script without a bit of finagling. Staying with the theme of strategic laziness, we recommend downloading the beautiful and user-friendly Jupyter Notebook for easy data visualization. As a word of warning, Jupyter Notebooks is an amazing tool for development, but we stress that it is not recommended that you deploy Jupyter scripts in a production environment. Jupyter's friendly

UI interface and easy visualization of code are due to its memory- and processing-heavy framework that is inevitably quite clunky and slow in a pipeline.

You can follow the instructions mentioned here to download and set up Jupyter Notebook: https://jupyter.org/install.

Next, we will document the environmental dependencies using a requirements.txt file.

Documenting environment dependencies with requirements.txt

Creating and maintaining a requirements.txt document is a standard practice in Python application development. Future updates or major changes to dependencies could potentially break the application, but developers can always install the recorded previous versions, ensuring smooth execution of the code without errors. By freezing the application to specific versions of dependencies, it ensures that, given the correct requirements, your project will maintain its original state. This approach proves beneficial, providing a win-win situation for developers and the application's reliability.

Let's look at how to install dependencies using the requirements.txt file:

```
(base) usr@project%    pip install -r requirements.txt
ex: requirements.txt


pip==3.9
python==3.9.4
pandas==1.4.2
requests==2.28.0
```

Additionally, you can update and store the new package imports and versions with the following command to keep the requirements.txt file up to date:

```
(base) usr@project %    pip freeze >> requirements.txt
```

That is how we can collect dependencies in the requirements.txt file. The next section will review some key concepts that are essential to know before we start building data pipelines.

Accounting for circular dependencies

The concept of circular dependency is not always talked about when first learning Python, but it's a concept where one or more modules depend on each other:

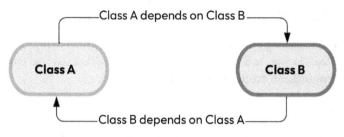

Figure 1.1: A circular dependency

While there are many useful aspects of this interdependency, underlying second and third-degree inconsistencies, such as one Python module version being incompatible with another Python module version, can result in a cascading effect of uncontrolled errors that lead to a smorgasbord of application failures. Alluding back to our initial analogy about a development project being similar to a laboratory experiment, this is why system *sterility* comes into play. To create an internally consistent environment, versions of the dependencies must be flexibly adjusted to account for the circular interdependencies of imports. This magic of MMS begins!

Utilizing module management systems (MMSs)

MMSs are like special folders that only work in certain environments. They do this by changing `sys.prefix` and `sys.exec_prefix` so that they point to the base directory of the virtual environment. This is helpful because it lets developers create "clean" applications and also makes sure that all the different parts of the project work well together.

There are many different module management systems to choose from, but Anaconda is the most popular. However, it doesn't always have the most up-to-date packages for data engineers, and `pip`, the regular package manager for Python, doesn't work well with Anaconda. That's why we're using `pipenv` in this book. It's a virtual environment and package management system that uses `Pipfile` and `Pipfile.lock`, similar to a `requirements.txt` file.

Instigating a virtual MMS environment within your local IDE

Creating a virtual MMS environment within your local IDE can be a helpful way to test and run your code before you implement it in a larger system. This virtual environment allows you to simulate different scenarios and conditions to ensure that your code is working properly and efficiently. It can also help you identify and fix any errors or bugs that may arise during the development process.

Overall, setting up a virtual MMS environment within your local IDE can be a valuable tool for streamlining your coding workflow and ensuring that your projects are successful.

Configuring a Pipenv environment in PyCharm

In Python development, managing project environments is crucial to keep your project's dependencies organized and controlled. One way to achieve this is by using pipenv. Let's start the process by installing Pipenv. Open your Terminal and execute the following command:

```
(base) usr@project %    pip install --user pipenv
```

This command instructs `pip` (a Python package manager) to install Pipenv in your user space. The `--user` option ensures that Pipenv is installed in the user install directory for your platform.

After successful installation, this is what your Terminal should look like:

```
    100% |                                  |  6.4MB 220kB/s
Collecting virtualenv (from pipenv)
   Downloading https://files.pythonhosted.org/packages/b6/30/96a02b2287098b23b875bc8c2f58071c3
5d2efe84f747b64d523721dc2b5/virtualenv-16.0.0-py2.py3-none-any.whl (1.9MB)
    100% |                                  |  1.9MB 420kB/s
Requirement already satisfied: pip>=9.0.1 in c:\python37\lib\site-packages (from pipenv)
Requirement already satisfied: certifi in c:\python37\lib\site-packages (from pipenv)
Collecting virtualenv-clone>=0.2.5 (from pipenv)
   Downloading https://files.pythonhosted.org/packages/6d/c2/dccb5ccf599e0c5d1eea6acbd058af7a7
1384f9740179db67a9182a24798/virtualenv_clone-0.3.0-py2.py3-none-any.whl
Requirement already satisfied: setuptools>=36.2.1 in c:\python37\lib\site-packages (from pipe
nv)
Installing collected packages: virtualenv, virtualenv-clone, pipenv
Successfully installed pipenv-2018.5.18 virtualenv-16.0.0 virtualenv-clone-0.3.0
You are using pip version 9.0.1, however version 10.0.1 is available.
You should consider upgrading via the 'python -m pip install --upgrade pip' command.
```

Figure 1.2: Command-line view of installing pipenv

Once installed, remember to activate the `pipenv` environment before you begin to work on your new project. This way, the entirety of your project is developed within the isolated virtual environment.

Each time you activate `pipenv`, the command line will display the following:

```
(base) usr@project %    pipenv shell

Creating a virtualenv for this project...
Pipfile: /Users/usr/project/Pipfile
Using /Users/usr/.pyenv/versions/3.10.4/bin/python3 (3.10.4) to create
virtualenv...

⋮ Creating virtual environment...created virtual environment
CPython3.10.4.final.0-64 in 903ms
   creator CPython3Posix(dest=/Users/usr/.local/share/virtualenvs/
project-dGXB4pbM, clear=False, no_vcs_ignore=False, global=False)
   seeder FromAppData(download=False, pip=bundle, setuptools=bundle,
wheel=bundle, via=copy, app_data_dir=/Users/usr/Library/Application
Support/virtualenv)
```

```
    added seed packages: pip==22.1.2, setuptools==62.6.0,
wheel==0.37.1
    activators BashActivator,CShellActivator,FishActivator,
NushellActivator,PowerShellActivator,PythonActivator

✓ Successfully created virtual environment!
Virtualenv location: /Users/usr/.local/share/virtualenvs/TestFiles-
dGXB4pbM
Launching subshell in virtual environment...
 . /Users/usr/.local/share/virtualenvs/project-dGXB4pbM/bin/activate

(Project) usr@project %%   . /Users/usr/.local/share/virtualenvs/
project
-dGXB4pbM/bin/activate
```

Now that we have learned how to activate a virtual environment using pip, we can move on to installing packages within that environment.

Installing packages

pip- packages can be added or removed from the environment via simple $ pipenv install or $ pipenv uninstall commands since activating the pipenv environment is designed to replace the need for the pip- tag in the command line.

Pipfile and Pipfile.lock

When a pipenv environment is initiated, an empty Pipfile is automatically created. As mentioned previously, Pipfile is synonymous with the requirements.txt file.

Pipfile.lock is created to specify which version of the dependencies referenced in Pipfile should be used to avoid automatic upgrades of packages that depend on each other. You can run the $ pipenv lock command to update the Pipfile.lock file with the currently used versions of all the dependencies within your virtual environment. However, pipenv takes care of updating the Pipfile and Pipfile.lock files with each package installation.

The following example shows how we can use Pipfile and Pipfile.lock:

```
(Project) usr@project %%   pipenv install numba
Installing numba...
Adding numba to Pipfile's [packages]...
✓ Installation Succeeded
Pipfile.lock (aa8734) out of date, updating to (d71de2)...
Locking [dev-packages] dependencies...
Locking [packages] dependencies...
Building requirements...
Resolving dependencies...
```

```
✓ Success!
Updated Pipfile.lock (d71de2)!
Installing dependencies from Pipfile.lock (d71de2)...
🐍 ‖‖‖‖‖‖‖‖‖‖‖‖‖‖‖‖‖‖‖‖‖‖‖‖‖‖‖‖‖‖‖‖‖‖‖‖‖1/1 — 00
```

Now, let's summarize what we have learned in this chapter in the next section.

Summary

In this chapter, we learned about various data structures in Python, including if-else conditions and looping techniques. We also learned about functions and object-oriented programming in Python. Then, we covered working with files in Python, including version control with Git tracking and documenting environment dependencies with requirements.txt. Additionally, we learned about utilizing module management systems and instigating a virtual MMS environment within a local IDE. Finally, we covered installing packages and working with Pipfile and Pipfile.lock.

In the next chapter, we will discuss the concept of data pipelines and how to create robust ones, including the process of automating ETL pipelines and how to ensure that data is consistently and accurately moved and transformed. See you in *Chapter 2*!

2

Understanding the ETL Process and Data Pipelines

With a firm foundation of Python under our belts and a clean development environment established, we can now pivot to talking about the fundamentals of data pipelines.

Within this chapter, we will define what a data pipeline is, as well as take a more in-depth look at the process of building robust pipelines. We will then discuss different approaches, such as the **Extract, Transform, and Load** (ETL) and **Extract, Load, and Transform** (**ELT**) methodologies, and how they tie into effectively automating data movement.

By the end of this chapter, you will have an established workflow for building data pipelines within your local environment and will have covered the following topics:

- What is a data pipeline?
- Creating robust data pipelines
- What is an ETL pipeline? How do ETL pipelines differ from ELT pipelines?
- Automating ETL pipelines
- Examples of use cases of ETL pipelines

What is a data pipeline?

A data pipeline is a series of tasks, such as transformations, filters, aggregations, and merging multiple sources, before outputting the processed data into some target. In layman's terms, a data pipeline gets data from the "source" to the "target," as depicted in the following diagram:

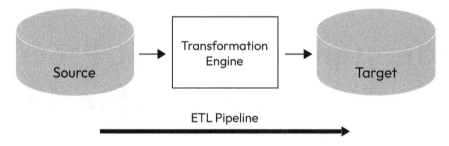

Figure 2.1: A sample ETL process illustration

You can think of pipelines as transport tubes in a mailroom. Mail can be placed in specific tubes and *sucked* up to specific processing centers. Based on specific labels, the mail is then moved and sorted into specific pathways that eventually bring it to its destination. The core concept of data pipelines is quite similar. Like mail, packets of raw data are ingested into the entry of the pipeline and, through a series of steps and processes, the raw material is formatted and packaged into an output location, which is most commonly used for storage.

From a business perspective, the driving incentive for creating data pipelines is to design a system to transform their most valuable asset – raw data – into actionable information (*Reference #2*). Typically, data pipeline architectures feature a unidirectional (one-way) communication flow between the flow of input data sources to output data storage systems (*Reference #1*):

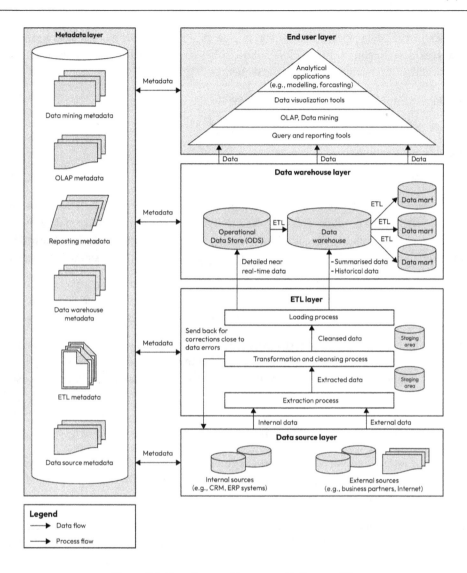

Figure 2.2: Data flow architecture – (Reference #1)

Now that we have a clearer picture of the general structure of a data pipeline, we can dive into what makes a data pipeline *robust* and what doesn't.

How do we create a robust pipeline?

A data pipeline is only as scalable as its foundation is strong. It is crucial to meticulously design an architectural plan, which includes anything from defining the types of data that need to be collected to the methodologies used to analyze the data, to create a sustainable data environment

(*Reference #2*). Just as a data pipeline built with a strong architecture is easily maintainable and scalable, so too is a weak data pipeline at high risk of failure, either structurally or analytically producing an inaccurate product, and having staggering consequences.

The following are the attributes of a robust data pipeline:

- Clearly defined expectations
- Scalable architecture
- Reproducible and clear

A robust data pipeline should have clearly defined expectations in terms of the data it is processing and the results it is expected to produce. This includes specifying the types and sources of data, as well as the desired output format and any required transformations or aggregations. Having clearly defined expectations helps ensure that the pipeline is consistently producing accurate and reliable results.

In addition to clearly defined expectations, a robust data pipeline should have a scalable architecture that can handle increasing volumes of data without degradation in performance. This may involve using distributed systems or implementing efficient algorithms to process the data promptly.

Reproducibility and clarity are also important attributes of a robust data pipeline. The pipeline should be able to produce the same results each time it is run, and the steps involved in processing the data should be documented and easy to understand. This helps ensure that the pipeline can easily be maintained and modified as needed.

Pre-work – understanding your data

Your data is your foundation. It's what dictates the context and flow of the overall data pipeline. As the designer of the pipeline, it is best to become intimately familiar with both the input and output data structure requirements, as follows:

- **Input data**: You should write clear definitions of the input data, such as its data structures, the prevalence of corrupted data, and the frequency of new data creation. What is the likelihood of data corruption, and how can it be accounted for within the pipeline?
- **Output data**: It is important to have a thorough understanding of the structural requirements of the output data to ensure that the project's goals are consistently upheld during its design and construction. A weak pipeline is problematic, but a pipeline that serves no purpose is even worse. It is crucial to achieve the desired result; otherwise, the entire effort becomes pointless.

In summary, it is important to have a clear understanding of both the input and output data structures when designing a data pipeline. This includes knowing the data structures, any potential issues with the data (such as corruption), and the frequency of new data creation for the input data. For the output data, it is important to understand the structural requirements to ensure that the pipeline consistently produces the desired result. It is also important to ensure that the pipeline serves a purpose and helps achieve the project's goals. If the pipeline does not produce the desired result or serve a purpose, it may be considered pointless.

Design planning – planning your workflow

Before writing a line of code, take some time to sketch out a flowchart of the transformations that need to be performed on the input data to produce the output data. Go a little deeper into how Python packages can be used to accomplish these transformations. This is how you create the foundation for operational stability in your code, where you apply **Don't Repeat Yourself** (**DRY**) practices to create non-redundant code that is thoroughly tested and easy to logically follow.

DRY practices are a programming principle that aims to reduce redundancy in code. This means avoiding writing the same code multiple times, and instead using functions, variables, and other code structures to reuse code whenever possible.

Architecture development – developing your resources

As the architect responsible for the data pipeline, you need to understand the various types of connections needed to securely link the source(s) of your input data to your development and production environments, as well as the method for connecting to the output location. You will also need to determine the approach for your pipeline and the level of error handling necessary to ensure the long-term stability and reliability of the pipeline.

This is the *meat and potatoes* of the true purpose of a data engineer, and it's a *massive* topic. Don't worry – we will delve more deeply into this topic in *Part 2*.

Putting it all together – project diagrams

Arguably, this is where our methods might diverge a bit from the norm. As strong advocates for *strategic laziness*, getting your entire workflow on paper is an incredibly effective tool for communicating your desired results to both yourself and others. Creating project diagrams is fundamental to a project that is not only clear, reproducible, and fully strategized, but also makes it highly shareable and transparent.

Utilizing visual aids can greatly help with efficiently processing information for most people, making it simple for you to communicate your pipelines to non-technical individuals. This is where you put all of the previous steps together, and add details around each component of the pipeline's workflow to establish what needs to be designed to create the desired output data, in the desired format and storage endpoint.

The following diagram illustrates the end-to-end process of data processing, including the final utilization of the data:

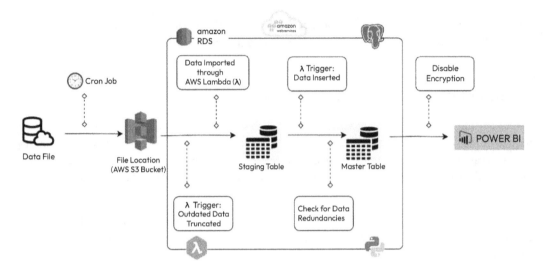

Figure 2.3: Data processing with ETL

Now that we have a deep understanding of the elements that make up a strong data pipeline, let's delve into the various architectural approaches for constructing robust pipelines.

What is an ETL data pipeline?

ETL stands for **Extract**, **Transform**, and **Load**. In an ELT process, data is first extracted from a source, then transformed and formatted in a specific way, and finally loaded into a final storage location. These pipelines are useful for organizing and preparing data for future purposes such as performing analysis and model creation smoothly and efficiently:

ETL PIPELINE

Figure 2.4: Sample ETL pipeline

ELT stands for **Extract**, **Load**, and **Transform**, and is similar to ETL, but the data is first loaded into the target system and then transformed within the target system.

Which one to use depends on the specific requirements and characteristics of the systems involved and the data being moved. Here are a few factors that you might consider when deciding between ETL and ELT:

- **Data volume**: If the volume of data is very large, ELT might be more efficient because the transformation step can be done in parallel within the target system

- **Data transformation requirements**: If the data needs to undergo complex transformations, it might be easier to perform the transformations in the target system using ELT

- **Source system capabilities**: If the source system is not able to perform the necessary transformations, ETL might be the only option

- **Target system capabilities**: If the target system is not able to efficiently handle the load phase of the ETL process, ELT might be a better option

- **Data latency**: If real-time data movement is required, ELT might be a better choice because it allows the data to be loaded and transformed more quickly

In general, ETL is more commonly used when the source and target systems are different and the data needs to be transformed in a specific way before it is loaded into the target system. ELT is more commonly used when the target system is more powerful and can handle the transformation step itself:

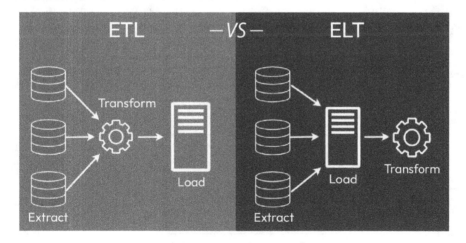

Figure 2.5: ETL versus ELT

In this book, we will focus more exclusively on ETL pipelines, where there are clear output data expectations.

There are three main types of ETL pipelines:

- Batch processing
- Streaming
- Cloud-native

Let's take a look!

Batch processing

Batch processing is a method of data processing that involves dividing a large volume of data into smaller pieces, or batches, and processing each batch separately. This is often done when a project requires a large amount of data to be handled (mostly in TB or above), but the downstream use of the data only requires it to be available asynchronously. Batch processing is a popular choice for handling large amounts of data because it allows engineers to design a process that can run one batch of data through the pipeline at a time, rather than trying to process all of the data at once. This is especially useful for moving large amounts of data at regular intervals.

One example of a batch processing system is a company that processes customer orders for an online store. The company receives a large volume of orders each day and needs to process this data to update inventory levels, generate invoices, and fulfill orders. To do this, they use a batch processing system to break the data into smaller chunks and run each chunk through their data pipeline. This allows them to process the data efficiently, without overwhelming their systems or causing delays in order processing:

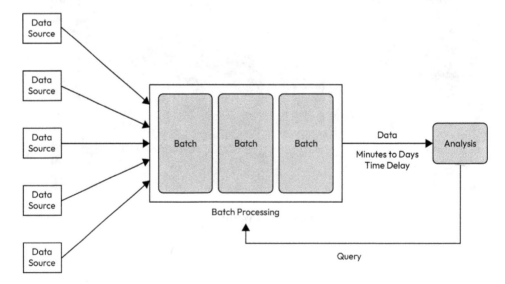

Figure 2.6: An illustration of batch processing

An example of this is ingesting the user's data from an e-commerce website every 30 minutes and passing it through a pipeline to transform and load it into **relational database management system (RDBMS)** tables in a data warehousing setup.

Streaming method

Real-time data solutions are necessary when a project needs to immediately process fresh data. Streaming methods are often used in these situations as they allow data to flow continuously, which may be variable and subject to sudden changes in structure. To handle these challenges, a combination of data pipelines is typically utilized. There are several advanced tools, such as Apache Storm and Apache Samza, that can efficiently process real-time data. We will delve further into this topic in future chapters.

An example of this is an e-commerce website that needs to process real-time user data as shopping is in progress. The use of real-time data processing, combined with AI/ML, can result in an enhanced user shopping experience.

Cloud-native

After the advent of cloud technologies, complex data processing has become very easy. Most of the famous public cloud platforms, such as **Amazon Web Services (AWS)**, **Google Cloud Platform (GCP)**, and **Microsoft Azure**, provide in-built data processing capabilities that come with various integrated tools and technologies that can be used to build a robust and resilient ETL pipeline.

Putting it all together

ETL and ELT are data processing approaches that involve extracting data from a source, performing transformations on it, and loading it into a final storage location. ETL is commonly used when the source and target systems are different and the data needs to be transformed in a specific way before it is loaded into the target system. ELT is more commonly used when the target system is more powerful and can handle the transformation step itself. Factors to consider when deciding between ETL and ELT include data volume, transformation requirements, source and target system capabilities, and data latency. There are three main types of ETL pipelines: batch processing, streaming, and cloud-native. Batch processing is used for large volumes of data that only need to be available asynchronously, streaming is used for real-time data processing, and cloud-native is used for data processing in cloud computing environments. The purpose of this book is to focus on ETL pipelines where there are clear output data expectations.

Next, we will explore the process of automating ETL pipelines.

Automating ETL pipelines

To streamline and optimize the ETL process in a production environment, there are several tools and technologies available to automate the pipeline. These tools are particularly important in an enterprise setting, where the volume and complexity of data can be significant. In this section, we will discuss the most important and relevant tools used in an enterprise environment.

There are several key benefits to automating ETL pipelines:

- **Data democratization**: Automating the ETL process can make it easier for a wider range of users to access and use data since the process of extracting, transforming, and loading data is streamlined and made more efficient

- **Robust data availability and access**: By automating the ETL process, data is made more consistently available and accessible to users since the pipelines are designed to run regularly and can be easily configured to handle any changes or updates to the source data

- **Team focus**: Automating ETL pipelines can free up team members to focus on more important tasks such as data analytics, developing machine learning models, and other higher-value activities, rather than spending time on manual data preparation tasks

- **Onboarding process**: Automated ETL pipelines can make it easier and faster to onboard new team members since the process of extracting and preparing data is already streamlined and automated, reducing the need for new hires to learn complex manual processes

- **Schema management**: Automating ETL pipelines can also help with schema management since the pipelines can be configured to handle changes to the source data schema automatically, ensuring that the data is always properly transformed and loaded into the target system

By utilizing tools such as AWS Lambda and EC2 alongside Step Functions, it is simple to orchestrate or automate ETL pipelines on a cloud platform. For instance, we can implement these resources to automate our pipelines effectively.

Orchestrating ETL pipelines can also be done using open source tools such as Apache Airflow, Luigi, and others (more on this in *Parts 2 and 3*).

Exploring use cases for ETL pipelines

Now, we will cover the benefits and uses of ETL pipelines in organizations:

- Benefits of ETL pipelines:

  - Allow developers and engineers to focus on useful tasks rather than worrying about data

  - Free up time for developers, engineers, and scientists to focus on actual work

  - Help organizations move data from one place to another and transform it into a desired format efficiently and systematically

- Applications of ETL pipelines:

  - Migrating data from a legacy platform to the cloud and vice versa

  - Centralizing data sources to have a consolidated view of data

  - Providing stable data sources for data-driven applications and data analytic tools

  - Acting as a blueprint for organizational data, serving as a single source of truth

- Example of an ETL pipeline in action:

  - Netflix has a very robust ETL pipeline that manages petabytes of data, allowing them to employ a small team of engineers to handle admin tasks related to data

- Overall benefits of ETL pipelines:

  - Saves money in the long run

  - Helps with business expansion

With that, we have come to the end of this chapter.

Summary

In this chapter, we learned about data pipelines and the ETL process, as well as the different approaches and types of ETL pipelines, including batch processing, streaming, and cloud-native. We also learned about the benefits of automating ETL pipelines, such as schema management and data quality. In the next chapter, we will learn about the process of creating a scalable and resilient pipeline.

References

To learn more about the topics that were covered in this chapter, take a look at the following resources:

1. *ETL and its impact on Business Intelligence*: https://www.academia.edu/11434594/ETL_and_its_impact_on_Business_Intelligence?email_work_card=title

2. *A Five-Layered Business Intelligence Architecture*: https://www.academia.edu/25962611/A_Five_Layered_Business_Intelligence_Architecture?email_work_card=view-paper

3

Design Principles for Creating Scalable and Resilient Pipelines

The true art of data engineering is the architecture of the pipeline design. This chapter deals with the implementation of the most effective design patterns and the top open source Python libraries used to create an enterprise-grade ETL pipeline. It illustrates how to install these libraries and has primers on all the functions available to create robust pipelines. This also explains all the design patterns and approaches available to create the ETL process.

By the end of this chapter, you will have an established workflow for building data pipelines within your local environment in the following ways:

- Understanding the design patterns for ETL pipelines
- Preparing your local environment for installations
- Open source Python libraries for ETL pipelines

Technical requirements

For the rest of the book, we will be using Pipenv, PyCharm, and Jupyter Notebook for local development and version control with a Git-tracked repository. To empower yourself to follow along with the coding examples and tutorials, we highly encourage you to revisit *Chapter 1*, to walk through the instructions to download and install each tool in your local environment and fork your own variation of the Git repository associated with this book.

Assuming you're ready to go, let's get started on setting up our virtual environment for development! Open up your PyCharm application, select **Get from VCS**, and clone your GitHub repository into your PyCharm environment. Within the project, open up the PyCharm terminal and run the following commands:

```
(base) usr@project %   pipenv shell
```

Understanding the design patterns for ETL

Even though the term was coined in 1958, **business intelligence (BI)** is a rather new discipline with a lot of research activity; its popularity in information systems has only gained popularity in the last few years (*Reference #1*). This rapid progress has also brought a high level of heterogeneity of several approaches for effective design patterns for data movement processes and design pattern norms within specific institutions (*Reference #2*). Thus, the formation of standardized, reliable, roadmaps for BI progress has slowly taken shape over time. The **Extract, Transform, and Load (ETL)** perspective for data pipelines has helped shaped the complexity of BI activities into neat building blocks to identify and represent frequently recurring patterns within an organization's scope of data movement needs.

We chose to write this book from the *plug and play* perspective, which is why we chose to focus on the most common and versatile ETL design patterns. This way, even in complex environments, you will, at the very least, gain the perspective to create effective proof-of-concept data pipelines that can be built upon with more complex methodologies downstream. Let's dive in!

Basic ETL design pattern

Starting off short and sweet, you can examine the following diagram of the most basic and simplest ETL pipeline design:

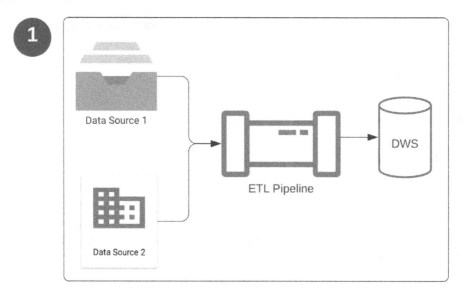

Figure 3.1: Single-layer ETL design pattern

Reading from right to left, you see one or two data sources that are fed into an ETL process that records the resulting data in one **data warehouse** (**DWS** in the diagram) location. This is a great place to start when designing the general flow of data "from A to B" so you can easily separate each "Import-Process-Export" step into a different process. But what happens when a network issue occurs mid-operation? What happens to the data in the middle of the pipeline? Is any data retained? It quickly becomes clear that things get a little hairy for basic pipeline designs when anything but perfect conditions arises. Single process ETL patterns as in *Figure 3.1* are quite rigid, typically flowing from start to finish in one go, and take little to no precautions for lapses in data migration activities; if the connection is lost mid-stream, so is the data in between. This alludes to some quite costly contingencies when seeking scale (a data pipeline beyond its preliminary scope) since redundant processing power is required to redo any data transactions lost in a network failure. Thus, there is a pressing need for intermittent data storage.

ETL-P design pattern

To address some of the data loss and processing power challenges found in the most basic ETL design, engineers added a **Persistent Staging Area** (**PSA**) layer to the pipeline to preserve segments of data source conversions during the data migration, even if the source system is facing network or latency issues. Check out the following diagram:

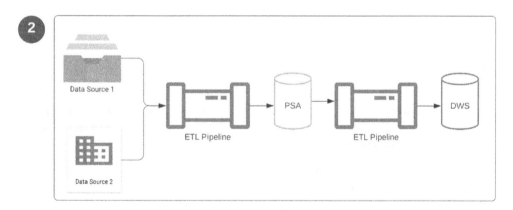

Figure 3.2: ETL-P design pattern (with PSA layer)

Specifically, the PSA layer breaks up the data importation and data exportation stages to limit the liability of data movement issues from the connection between the source and sink data locations being severed. In practice, staging locations have a wide variety of applications and use cases, so we like to think of this as a "sanity check" step. For instance, some organizations store a master staging file to measure the data integrity of fresh data imports with the existing data expectations of the system. However, what happens if the connection to the data source is inconsistent, or on a different frequency than what's needed for the business needs for data ingestion? The PSA layer alone can't accommodate this need; it looks like there's a need for an additional layer.

ETL-VP design pattern

With an added **volatile staging area** (**VSA**) layer, the ETL-VP is the glow-up version of the ETL-P pipeline design pattern, as seen in the following diagram:

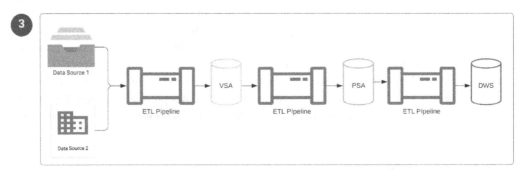

Figure 3.3: ETL-VP design pattern (with VSA and PSA layers)

The ETL-VP can handle asynchronous data importation processes with ease due to its ability to use the VSA layer to batch-load data into the PSA layer on a predictable and consistent schedule. This additional layer also further minimizes the impact of network connectivity issues by maintaining the ETL's performance at a predictable frequency. However, as engineers, there's always one nagging curiosity: "It works, but can we make this better?" Yes, we can.

ELT two-phase pattern

The full scope two-phase ETL design pattern is the crème de la crème. While the ELT-VP compensates for many connectivity issues, it is a high computational investment to sync the data loading process with the data collection process. In other words, it can become a money-munging machine. Let's examine the following diagram:

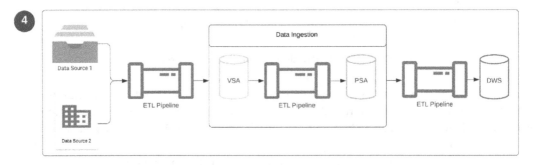

Figure 3.4: Two-phase ETL design pattern (with VSA and PSA layers)

As it turns out, breaking the collection of sources and the loading of data into separate steps is a handy way to reduce some of these preventable costs. Building a data pipeline in this fashion gives more control over the pipeline as well as makes each process more dynamic and reusable, as the same method for data importation can be used with customizable and interchangeable methods of loading the data with various other filters and audit mechanisms.

With a better understanding of the structure, as well as the pros and cons, of some of the most common ETL design patterns, let's get into the practical construction of these pipelines in code. However, before diving into the construction of ETL pipelines in raw Python, we thought it was pertinent to review best practices for your pipeline coding environment. In the next section, we will take some time to walk through setting up your environment with some of the standard Python modules that are used to create dynamic ETL pipelines.

Preparing your local environment for installations

Back in *Chapter 1*, we reviewed the relationship between `pip` package imports and the `pipenv` virtual environment. This is echoed in the syntax for Python module management from the command line, which is added or removed from the environment with simple `$ pipenv install` or `$ pipenv uninstall` commands.

> **Note**
> You *must* use this syntax when installing packages to keep the packages locally installed within your `pipenv` environment for this project.

Open source Python libraries for ETL pipelines

If you're familiar with the Python programming language, you're probably already acquainted with Pandas and NumPy, two of Python's currently most-used modules for processing various sources of data. For those of you who are less acquainted, we have provided a brief overview of both packages next.

Pandas

In the wild, giant pandas adapted vertical pupils (similar to cats) that enable them to have amazing night vision. It's useful to think of Python modules, such as Pandas, in the same context as evolutionary adaptations. Modules such as Pandas are specific augmentations to programming languages such as Python, which make completing tasks not only easier to perform but typically with more clarity and less code.

Similar to its furry counterpart, the Pandas Python module is powerful and flexible, and it was designed to be as close to a one-stop shop for processing data files as reasonably possible. Imported with the `pd` prefix, the Pandas library contains the most common import functions for data sources (such as CSV,

YXY, and Excel) with simple, human-readable commands such as `pd.read_csv(file__path)`. It's also the most effective for merging data sources together or aggregating data to desirable levels.

Pandas is a nice plug and play module that is easily installed directly on your local environment (though for the purpose of this book, we highly recommend downloading within your virtual `pipenv` environment – more on that later).

It's important to keep in mind that most Python modules rely on the CPUs available on your local device, which means that one problem with Pandas is its processing capacity. When data is imported with Pandas, the data is stored in the local memory on your device during the duration of the script. This becomes problematic, and very quickly, as multiple data copies are created of larger and larger datasets, even if only during a script's cycle.

Feel free to comb through the documentation for more information about Pandas: `https://pypi.org/project/pandas/`.

Within your virtual environment, please execute the following command to install Pandas into your project environment. We provided the full installation output so you can get more familiar with what `pipenv` outputs for successful package installation:

```
(Project) usr@project %%  pipenv install pandas
Installing pandas...
Adding pandas to Pipfile's [packages]..
√ Installation Succeeded
Pipfile.lock not found, creating
Locking [dev-packages] dependencies
Locking [packages] dependencies
Building requirements
Resolving dependencies
√ Success!
Updated Pipfile.lock (950830)!
Installing dependencies from Pipfile.lock (950830)
   🐍 ||||||||||||||||||||||||||||||||||  0/0 — 0
```

NumPy

When it comes to crunching numbers, NumPy is your guy. NumPy is a conjunction of "Numbers + Python" and was designed by mathematicians and statisticians that like to keep the mathematical jargon (and therefore integrity) under the pretty hood of a lovely np abbreviation. Like Pandas, NumPy is also a quick start package install when initiating a new script for data processing, as NumPy can be used for anything ranging from defining and converting data types within a data structure to merging multiple data sources into one clear, mathematically correct aggregate. Also like Pandas, NumPy can easily run on your local environment. For a more in-depth overview of NumPy, feel free to reference the documentation: `https://pypi.org/project/numpy/`.

In your virtual environment, please execute the following command to install NumPy into your project environment. Similar to the Pandas installation previously, the `Pipfile.Lock` file is updated as part of each new package installation:

```
(Project) usr@project %%  pipenv install numpy
Installing numpy
Adding numpy to Pipfile's [packages]
✓ Installation Succeeded
Pipfile.lock (950830) out of date, updating to (1c7351)
Locking [dev-packages] dependencies
Locking [packages] dependencies
Building requirements
Resolving dependencies
✓ Success!
Updated Pipfile.lock (1c7351)!
Installing dependencies from Pipfile.lock (1c7351)
🐍  ||||||||||||||||||||||||||||||||||  0/0 — 0
```

Pandas and NumPy are both incredibly powerful and useful Python packages, but they have their limitations. Both Pandas and NumPy require a contiguous allocation of memory, thus, simple data manipulation operations become quite costly as each new version of the data is stored in contiguous memory locations. Even in large-capacity environments, both packages perform rather poorly (and unbearably slow) on large datasets. Since the premise of this book is creating reliable, scalable, data pipelines, restricting our code base to Pandas and NumPy simply won't do.

Scaling for big data packages

In this section, we will look at different tools that will help us with scaling the ETL pipelines for big data packages.

Dask

When faced with processing capacity contingencies, it makes sense to increase your capacity with the assistance of additional devices. This is the premise for the parallelization of tasks in Python. Similar to batch processing, partitioning data (aka separating the data into equal, bite-sized bits), allows large data sources to be processed in identical, synchronous ways across multiple systems.

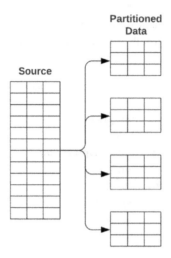

Figure 3.5: Concept of partitioning data

Dask is the Python library that allows for the parallelization of processing tasks in a flexible and dynamic scope. Dask is a cloud-based module that uses "clusters", which are extra processing units in the cloud on standby, that can lend a helping hand to heavy-processing tasks initiated on your local device. The creators of Dask designed this parallelization module to be an extension of popular data processing modules, such as Pandas and NumPy, so Dask's syntax mimics the same format. In the following figure, we provided some examples from Dask's documentation:

Dask DataFrame mimics Pandas - documentation

```
import pandas as pd                      import dask.dataframe as dd
df = pd.read_csv('2015-01-01.csv')       df = dd.read_csv('2015-*-*.csv')
df.groupby(df.user_id).value.mean()      df.groupby(df.user_id).value.mean().compute()
```

Dask Array mimics NumPy - documentation

```
import numpy as np                       import dask.array as da
f = h5py.File('myfile.hdf5')             f = h5py.File('myfile.hdf5')
x = np.array(f['/small-data'])           x = da.from_array(f['/big-data'],
                                                          chunks=(1000, 1000))
x - x.mean(axis=1)                       x - x.mean(axis=1).compute()
```

Figure 3.6: Example of Dask's familiar user interface (source: https://docs.dask.org/en/stable/)

The Dask library is an incredibly powerful and ubiquitous tool, but it can be equally as complex to get properly acquainted with. While we will intermittently review the core uses of Dask throughout the remainder of this book, we encourage you to take some time and go through the tutorials available within Dask's documentation to explore more complex applications: https://pypi.org/project/dask/.

Please install Dask into your virtual environment with the following code before moving to the next section:

```
(Project) usr@project %% pipenv install dask
```

Numba

Similar to Dask, Numba is another powerhouse module specifically designed to enhance numerical processes in Python. One of the main complaints about data processing in Python is its overall speed, even without dealing with big data files. This is partially due to Python's "preference" to wait to compile data before a command is executed. Numba uses a **just-in-time** (**JIT**) compilation (also dynamic translation), which brings Python processing speeds to be more in line with its humble C/C++ beginnings. With Numba, there's no need to run a separate compilation step; all you need to do is add Numba decorators before a Python function, and Numba does the rest:

```
from numba import njit
import random

@njit
def monte_carlo_pi(nsamples):
    acc = 0
    for i in range(nsamples):
        x = random.random()
        y = random.random()
        if (x ** 2 + y ** 2) < 1.0:
            acc += 1
    return 4.0 * acc / nsamples
```

Figure 3.7: Example of Numba's familiar user interface (source: https://numba.pydata.org/)

Numba works well with basic Python libraries such as Pandas and NumPy, distributed execution frameworks such as Dask, and Python development environment tools such as Jupyter notebooks, so we will dive more deeply into the use cases of Numba throughout the remainder of the book. Please install Numba into your virtual environment with the following code:

```
(Project) usr@project %% pipenv install numba
```

Feel free to check out more in the Numba documentation: https://pypi.org/project/numba/.

Summary

In this chapter, we went over the broad strokes of ETL pipeline design patterns, and the purpose of each layer of the respective design pattern. We then used the bulk of the chapter to prepare your environment for powerful Python modules that we'll use to implement ETL pipeline designs in raw Python code. With the stage set, your local environment primed for development, and with an introduction to how we plan to utilize each module in our pipeline designs, we can move on to creating ETL pipelines in Python. In *Chapter 4*, we'll start by getting into the nitty gritty details of sourcing insightful data for your pipeline, including some of the industry-standard strategies for data extraction.

References

The following are the references that we used in this chapter:

- *Reference 1*: Nitin Anan, *ETL and its impact on Business Intelligence*, International Journal of Scientific and Research Publications, Volume 4, Issue 2, February 2014 1ISSN 2250-3153

    ```
    https://www.academia.edu/11434594/ETL_and_its_impact_on_Business_
    Intelligence?email_work_card=title
    ```

- *Reference 2*: Theodorou, Vasileios, et al. *Frequent patterns in ETL workflows: An empirical approach.* Data Knowl. Eng. 112 (2017): 1-16.

    ```
    https://upcommons.upc.edu/bitstream/handle/2117/110172/
    DATAK_2016_201_Revision+1_V0.pdf;jsessionid=0B98AFF1323933
    E58ABA42D6CC2C4304?sequence=4
    ```

Part 2: Designing ETL Pipelines with Python

For the second part of this book, we will get into the data extraction, transformation, and loading activities within ETL data pipelines. We will start by going over how to extract data from various source systems, from files to APIs to databases. After that, we will deal with various data transformation techniques in Python, and then end by looking into some of the best practices for data loading. We close out this section by exploring various open source Python tools that you can use to enhance the efficiency and design of your data pipelines.

This section contains the following chapters:

- *Chapter 4, Sourcing Insightful Data and Data Extraction Strategies*
- *Chapter 5, Data Cleansing and Transformation*
- *Chapter 6, Loading Transformed Data*
- *Chapter 7, Tutorial – Building an End-to-End ETL Pipeline in Python*
- *Chapter 8, Powerful ETL Libraries and Tools in Python*

4

Sourcing Insightful Data and Data Extraction Strategies

After reviewing the fundamentals of ETL pipelines and introducing powerful ETL modules in Python for creating data pipelines, we're now ready to write some code.

During this chapter, we will hop into the specifics of dealing with sourcing data from different types of systems and look at why combining various data sources within your pipeline is the secret sauce to successful data projects. Welcome to the beginning of the action!

In this chapter, we will cover the following topics:

- What is data sourcing?
- Accessibility to data
- Types of data sources
- Getting started with data extraction
- Creating a data extraction pipeline using Python

Technical requirements

You will find all code files required to follow along with this chapter in the respective chapter folder at `https://github.com/PacktPublishing/Building-ETL-Pipelines-with-Python`.

What is data sourcing?

Data sourcing refers to connecting your pipeline environment to all data input sources relevant to your data pipeline. Many applications require the use of structured data, as well as unstructured and semi-structured data, to make effective and timely decisions. This is depicted in the following diagram:

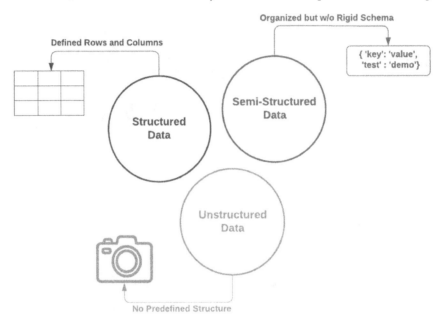

Figure 4.1 – Structured, semi-structured, and unstructured data definitions

All this data can be acquired from two types of sources: internal and external, where internal data refers to sources related to a company's business operations and external data refers to any data sourced outside of an organization (see *Reference #1* in the *References* section). While these terms are relative to the specific context of the organization and may or may not come into play for your own data pipeline projects, integrating both internal and external data helps produce an insightful, incredibly powerful output data product that can shed light on a powerful new perspective. Additionally, it's good to keep in mind that using relative paths to refer to data locations is extremely common in this industry.

So, what kinds of data sources are we talking about? We live in the era of data, so there is no shortage of data created; the paradox of choice is nigh. The trick to effective data sourcing is to find high-quality data that is easily accessible and that actually provides the data necessary to construct your output data. That way, you design a system that takes only the needed selected data through the process and gets rid of all unnecessary noise. With correct identification of data sources, problems such as inconsistent information, difficulty in finding root causes, and issues of data isolation can be avoided (see *Reference #2* in the *References* section).

Accessibility to data

Even though there are many existing data sources, some of them might be inaccessible, unreliable, or irrelevant to the purpose of your pipeline. Further, measuring the accessibility of data sources is dependent on circumstances that are oftentimes outside of your direct control, such as procuring the right access credentials, assessing the finesse of a company's cybersecurity system, or simply having a limitation in your system's short-term storage capacity.

Whatever the unique limitations of data accessibility are, it needs to be accounted for within the design of your architecture since the ability to connect to data sources with consistency has heavy impacts on downstream workflows. Being aware of the frequency of connection for each data source is essential to not only choose the most accessible data source but also to help determine the cadence of certain analytics due to the restriction of how often various sources can be merged together.

Types of data sources

There is an inexhaustible list of possible data sources for pipelines, and as the industry continues to evolve, new kinds of data sources will become available. Currently, data files or databases—whether structured, semi-structured, or unstructured—can all be used as both data sources and data sink locations. However, it is important to keep in mind that the more flexible the data definitions are for the data used in your pipeline, the more difficult it will be to validate the data produced by the pipeline. In this chapter, we are going to use some of the most frequently used source systems in the industry, as follows:

- CSV/Excel files
- Parquet files
- APIs
- RDBMS databases
- HTML

Getting started with data extraction

We will be using open source data for CSV, Parquet, and APIs, as well as manually preparing data for RDBMS databases and HTML using public safety data from *NYC Open Data* (available at https://data.cityofnewyork.us).

Within your PyCharm terminal, verify that your `pipenv` virtual environment has been activated and open the Jupyter notebook associated with *Chapter 4*. In the first cell, import the `pandas` module into your notebook, like so:

```
# Import modules
import pandas as pd
```

CSV and Excel data files

Not surprisingly, stored data files are commonly used as an input data source for an **extract, transform, load** (ETL) pipeline. Data files can be sourced from anywhere, from locally stored files on your device to cloud storage filesystems. Even when primarily working with databases or external APIs, using physical files is a great way to use timestamped data with ease, which can come in handy during any temporary connection issues.

Download the 500 latest records from the *Motor Vehicle Collisions - Crashes* data from the *NYC Open Data* website by entering the following URL into your browser: `https://data.cityofnewyork.us/resource/h9gi-nx95.csv?$limit=500`. This will download a CSV file, `h9gi-nx95.csv`. Please save this file in the same directory as your Jupyter notebook.

In your notebook, run the second cell in the notebook to read the CSV data using Pandas' `pd.read_csv()` command as a `df` DataFrame, then select the first five rows of the DataFrame with `df.head()`.

Parquet data files

As with CSV and Excel, the Parquet format is a file type that contains data (table type). However, while CSV and Excel data is stored as a plain text file, Parquet actually stores data in its binary form. Unlike CSV files, which store data by row, Parquet files store data by column, which makes it easier to manipulate at the column level versus at the row level. In other words, Parquet vectorizes the data, which is why Parquet is the preferred data format when working with large, stored data files since vectorizing the data rapidly decreases computation time.

In order to process Parquet files, we need to import a Python package, `pyarrow`, that enables Pandas, NumPy, and other built-in Python packages to process vectorized data (documentation: `https://arrow.apache.org/docs/python/index.html`). In the terminal section of your PyCharm environment, install `pyarrow` into your `pipenv` environment, like so:

```
(Project) usr@project %  pipenv install pyarrow
```

Next, download the January 2022 *Yellow Taxi Trip Records* data from the *NYC Open Data* website by entering the following URL into your browser: `https://www1.nyc.gov/site/tlc/about/tlc-trip-record-data.page`. This downloads a Parquet file, `yellow_tripdata_2022-01.parquet`. Save this file in the same directory as your Jupyter notebook and CSV file.

In your notebook, run the third cell in the notebook to read the Parquet data using Pandas' `pd.read_parquet()` command as a `df_parquet` DataFrame, then select the first five rows of the DataFrame with `df_parquet.head()`.

API connections

API connections are the wonderful plug and play data sources of the world. With an easy API key, either public or private, data connections can be made with ease to external data sources. You can get API links for anything from Twitter (now, X) social media data to **Armed Conflict Location & Event Data** (ACLED) data, often for the wonderful price of "free." Data ingestion through APIs is an integral part of modern ETL pipeline development. We will see an example of reading data from an API response and loading it to a Pandas DataFrame. As a word of caution: API data sources are typically controlled by another company, so not only do you have no control over the quality of the data, but your use of the data is also usually tracked. Proceed accordingly.

For this example, we will be using one of the *NYC Open Data* website's public HTTP APIs, which publishes data in JSON format: `https://data.cityofnewyork.us/resource/h9gi-nx95.json?$limit=500`. We need to import a Python library, `certifi`, which contains "*Root Certificates for validating the trustworthiness of SSL certificates while verifying the identity of TLS hosts*" (documentation: `https://pypi.org/project/certifi/`). In the terminal section of your PyCharm environment, run the following command:

```
(Project) usr@project %  pipenv install certifi
```

The `urllib3` Python library is a user-friendly HTTP client in Python that helps with some of the "under the hood" processes of retrying requests and dealing with HTTP redirects (documentation: `https://pypi.org/project/urllib3/`). In the terminal section of your PyCharm environment, run the following command:

```
(Project) usr@project %  pipenv install urllib3
```

In your notebook, verify all of the following modules are present since each one plays a role in the importation of JSON data from a URL request. Here's how you can do that:

```
# Import API-related Python modules
import json
import certifi
import urllib3
from urllib3 import request
```

Define an `url` variable for the preceding *NYC Open Data* API URL, and check the API connection status using `http.request('GET',url).status`. An API connection status informs you what is happening with the request. Was it successful? Was it redirected? If it failed, why did it fail? Here are the most common status codes for HTTP GET requests:

Status Code	General Meaning
200	Successful connection
400	Error/bad request/incorrect data was sent
401	Authentication error
403	Access forbidden
404	Resource not found in server

Table 4.1: Common HTTP GET request status codes

As you can see from the preceding table, a status code of 200 is the only code displayed when the connection is successful. Any other status code should be an error that is visible and present, plus blocked from continuing through your script, as malformed API-HTTP code can open your environment to security threats. That's when you'll see the following conditional statement to verify the status code is 200 before moving forward:

```
if apt_status == 200:
```

Once the status code confirms a successful connection, you'll need to create a pool manager to read the API response. The Pool Manager is a request method that handles connection pooling, which means that once a request is made, each consecutive time the connection is requested, the Pool Manager reuses the original connection in cached memory. This becomes particularly important when making web requests that have a limited number of "allowed" connections per day.

In the notebook, notice the urllib3.PoolManager() function handles the credentials necessary for the web request. To import the data in the desired JSON format, the json.loads() function wraps the request call that's appended with the data.decode('utf-8') function. Finally, the JSON file is normalized to clean up the output.

Databases

There are two main categories of database systems: relational (RDBMS) and non-relational (non-RDBMS). RDBMSs, such as MySQL and Oracle, comprise structured data that is organized into rows and columns, which are structures that DataFrames in Pandas seek to represent. Non-RDBMSs, such as MongoDB, are considered unstructured since they lack the defined data table of their RDBMS counterparts. This lack of structure is why non-RDBMSs are incredibly useful because there are few limitations around what can be stored within their systems; anything from documents to images to binary data files and other files can be stored in non-RDBMSs.

While databases are much more common for industry-level pipelines, Python actually has its own relational database, SQLite DB, built into its installation package. Since this is a full-fledged database, we will use it in the next example to not waste precious RAM space installing other external databases. We identified the movies.sqlite SQLite file for the following section.

Data from web pages

Lastly, we chose to review data from HTML sources, since engineers often "scrape" or gather data from open source web pages to create data to ingest in ETL pipelines. We will use the following *Wikipedia* URL, `https://en.wikipedia.org/wiki/List_of_countries_by_GDP_(nominal)`, to scrape the **Gross Domestic Product (GDP)** economic data for all the countries in the list.

Creating a data extraction pipeline using Python

With a bit more familiarity around where to source data, let's put it in the context of an importation activity within a data pipeline workflow. We're going to use a Jupyter notebook for prototyping the final methodology we will eventually deploy within a Python script. The reasoning behind this is simple: Jupyter notebooks allow easy visualization, but can be quite clunky to deploy; Python scripts have less visualization access (it can be done, but not as effortlessly as in Jupyter) but can easily be used for deployment and various environments. In our case, we want to properly test and "sanity-check" the format of the imported source data. Later in the book, we'll show how, when we transcribe our code to a Python script, we gain access to PyCharm's powerful environment to easily test, log, and encrypt Python scripts.

Data extraction

Within your PyCharm environment for *Chapter 4*, verify that you have initiated your `pipenv` environment with the `pipenv shell` command. Create a directory, `extraction`, and a new Python file, `extraction_functional.py`.

In the section of your script, write the following code to import important modules for data extraction:

```python
# Import modules
import json
import sqlite3
import certifi
import pandas as pd
import urllib3
```

In the Jupyter notebook associated with this chapter, create one function for importing data from a CSV file and a Parquet file, respectively. Here, we provided a variation of this, but feel free to create your own. Then, repeat the same process for importing data from API sources, SQLite data, and web page data. Finally, create a function that imports all forms of data within one `main` function. Run the function in your notebook; you should see the following result:

```
  VendorID tpep_pickup_datetime    congestion_surcharge airport_fee
0    1      2022-01-01 00:35:40     2.5                  0.0
1    1      2022-01-01 00:33:43     0.0                  0.0
2    2      2022-01-01 00:53:21     0.0                  0.0
```

```
3    2    2022-01-01 00:25:21    2.5        0.0
4    2    2022-01-01 00:36:48    2.5        0.0
[5 rows x 19 columns]
```

Logging

Logging is an important part of code to catch errors or exceptions. In this chapter, we will introduce logging to make our code debuggable. Don't worry if this portion goes over your head; we will go more intimately into logging later on in *Chapter 14*.

To start, it's wise to create a universal logging configuration that can be used in all Python modules without writing the boilerplate codes. A log file can be used for many purposes, including—but not limited to—analyzing any failure or finding bugs in the code. The code shown next creates a custom config for logging that creates an `etl_pipeline.log` log file under the `logs` directory.

You may want to visit `https://docs.python.org/3/howto/logging.html` for more detail on logging.

Open the `extraction/__init__.py` file and verify that the `config.py` script is imported into the `init` file, as follows:

```
from config import log_config
log_config.log_config()
```

With the config file in place, open the following extraction script:

```
extraction/extraction_functional_enhanced.py
```

Take note of how the logging modules are referenced within the script. At the start of the script, a logger instance is defined, like so:

```
# define top level module logger
logger = logging.getLogger(__name__)
```

Next, within each data import function, a `logger` instance is defined to record information related to the new data. For this example, we included the number of rows within the data file using the `df.shape[0]` syntax:

```
logger.info(f'{file_name} : extracted {df.shape[0]} records
fromthefile')
```

If any issue, or exception, occurred during the data import into a Python DataFrame, a log exception is recorded with a reference to the exception error:

```
logger.exception( f'{file_name} : - exception {e} encountered while
extracting the file')
```

In the event that these data sources are to be used as the source data for downstream processes, the newly imported data import is recorded with the same logging information throughout the data extraction pipeline.

Let's go and run this code in the console:

```
(base) usr@project % python extraction/extraction_functional_enhanced.
py
(base) usr@project % python
Python 3.9.7 (default, Sep 16 2021, 08:50:36)
[Clang 10.0.0 ] :: Anaconda, Inc. on darwin
Type "help", "copyright", "credits" or "license" for more information.
>>> from extraction import extraction_functional_enhanced
>>> df_parquit,_,_,_,_ = extraction_functional_enhanced.extracted_
data()
>>> df_parquit.head()
```

We get the following result:

```
(base) Brijs-MBP:pipeline brij$ python
Python 3.9.7 (default, Sep 16 2021, 08:50:36)
[Clang 10.0.0 ] :: Anaconda, Inc. on darwin
Type "help", "copyright", "credits" or "license" for more information.
>>> from extraction import extraction_functional
>>> df_parquit,_,_,_,_ = extraction_functional.extracted_data()
>>> df_parquit.head()
   VendorID tpep_pickup_datetime  ... congestion_surcharge airport_fee
0         1  2022-01-01 00:35:40  ...                  2.5         0.0
1         1  2022-01-01 00:33:43  ...                  0.0         0.0
2         2  2022-01-01 00:53:21  ...                  0.0         0.0
3         2  2022-01-01 00:25:21  ...                  2.5         0.0
4         2  2022-01-01 00:36:48  ...                  2.5         0.0

[5 rows x 19 columns]
```

Figure 4.2: Example output of pipeline run from iTerm terminal

Just to verify if a log file is created, go to the `logs` folder, and you should see the `etl_pipeline.log` log file. You may want to verify the content of this log file to know how many logging instances there are.

Summary

By this point in the chapter, you should be familiar with some of the most common data type sources used within the data extraction phase of an ETL pipeline. The associated GitHub scripts related to this chapter provided you with examples of data importation functions for each of the most common data sources, as well as what it looks like to construct a basic data extraction function for all data types within a command-line runnable Python script. This chapter closed off by walking you through logging tags for each activity, and the importance of logging both successful importations as well as accepting any error exception that might have occurred given a failure to import a data type.

In the next chapter, we begin to dive into the true beauty of the ETL process: data transformation—the step where data, from one or many sources, is molded to clean, statistically manipulated output data, which is the entire purpose of a data pipeline.

References

The following are the references that we used in this chapter:

- *Reference 1*: Nitin Anan, *ETL and its impact on Business Intelligence*, International Journal of Scientific and Research Publications, Volume 4, Issue 2, February 2014. ISSN 2250-3153

  (https://www.academia.edu/11434594/ETL_and_its_impact_on_Business_Intelligence?email_work_card=title)

- *Reference 2*: In Lih Ong, Pei Hwa Siew, and Siew Fan Wong. "*A Five-Layered Business Intelligence Architecture*." IBIMA Publishing Communications of the IBIMA, Vol. 2011 (2011), Article ID 695619, 11 pages. DOI: 10.5171/2011.695619

  (https://ibimapublishing.com/articles/CIBIMA/2011/695619/695619.pd)

5

Data Cleansing and Transformation

The success of a data pipeline is measured by its ability to transform the input data into the required attributes of the output data. It's the finesse of the transformation stage that separates a nice toy pipeline from a powerful and impactful enterprise pipeline. The accuracy and optimization of data transformations are manifested via the use of methodical approaches to construct each task performed.

In this chapter, we will explore various data transformation techniques in Python, and how these techniques can be used to massage data into the desired format. You will walk away from this chapter with a firm basis in the following areas of data manipulation:

- Data cleansing and transformation
- The importance of accuracy and consistency
- Data cleansing with Python
- Workflow for data transformation
- Creating a data transformation activity in Python

As this book is geared toward creating data pipelines, we will be covering only a handful of **Pandas** methods for illustration purposes. It's advisable to go through Pandas' official documentation to learn the various methods that can be used during the data transformation.

Technical requirements

To effectively utilize the resources and code examples provided in this chapter, ensure that your system meets the following technical requirements:

- Software requirements:

  - **Integrated development environment (IDE)**: We recommend using **PyCharm** as the preferred IDE for working with Python, and we might make specific references to PyCharm throughout this chapter. However, you are free to use any Python-compatible IDE of your choice.

  - Jupyter Notebooks should be installed.

  - Python version 3.6 or higher should be installed.

  - Pipenv should be installed for managing dependencies.

- GitHub repository:

  The associated code and resources for this chapter can be found in the following GitHub repository: `https://github.com/PacktPublishing/Building-ETL-Pipelines-with-Python`. We recommend that you fork and clone the repository to your local machine.

Exploring data cleansing and transformation

The extraction process is needed to select data that is significant in supporting the creation of the desired output data. Most often, the "input" data is a collection of data sources that need to be combined and manufactured in some fashion to collectively create the requested output data. Due to the wide variety of data recording methods, data storage definitions, and other uncontrolled variations between data sources, substantial modifications need to be performed. This is referred to as data "cleansing" and "transformation," which occurs within the "transform" step in the **extract, transform, load (ETL)** or **extract, load, transform (ELT)** data pipeline structure.

Scrubbing your data

Data cleansing, also referred to as data cleaning or scrubbing, is a term used to describe the manipulation of source data. It is a fundamental aspect of data engineering since unprocessed data is often quite messy and needs specific modifications to create a high-quality data output. The data cleansing process involves identifying and correcting or removing errors, inaccuracies, and inconsistencies in datasets to improve their quality and reliability. For instance, in a dataset of customer information, you might find duplicate entries, incorrect or missing values, or data in inconsistent formats.

The Pandas library is a great place to start since it is a powerful tool for data cleansing. In the following example, you'll see that we have a DataFrame of integers with missing values. We want to "cleanse" the data by filling those missing values with the mean of the remaining values in the respective column:

```
import pandas as pd
import numpy as np

# Create a DataFrame of Integers with some missing values
df = pd.DataFrame({
    'A': [1, 2, np.nan, 4],
    'B': [5, np.nan, np.nan, 8],
    'C': [9, 10, 11, 12]
})

# Fill missing values with mean
df.fillna(df.mean(), inplace=True)
```

Once the data is properly "cleaned," it's ready to move into the transformation stage, where the source data is beautified to fit the structure of the output data. Thus, methodologies for data transformation can collectively be put into two categories, structural and aesthetic, which we'll discuss in the following section.

Data transformation

Data transformation is the process of converting data from one format or structure into another. This is often necessary when moving data between systems that use different data formats, or when preparing data for analysis. Common data transformation operations include normalization, aggregation, and generalization. For instance, suppose we have a DataFrame and we want to normalize the values in a column so they fall between 0 and 1. We can accomplish this with the following code:

```
# Suppose 'A' is the column we want to normalize
df['A'] = (df['A'] - df['A'].min()) / (df['A'].max() - df['A'].min())
```

This is a simple example of data transformation, but in practice, data engineers often need to perform much more complex transformations. These might involve joining multiple datasets, reshaping data, or applying complex functions to data. Often, the data also requires aesthetic changes, such as renaming columns or reformatting column values, to create a dataset that can be easily visualized by a (non-technical) business team. Remember, effective data cleansing and transformation are fundamental to ensuring the trustworthiness of your data pipelines. As the engineer, you are responsible for maintaining the accuracy and reliability of your data, since your output data can significantly impact the success of any downstream processes that end up using it.

Data cleansing and transformation in ETL pipelines

Creating dynamic data-cleaning processes is the quickest way to prevent redundancy in your code base. There's nothing more aggravating, or more wasteful, than creating duplicate activities that accomplish the same task but with one or two inconsequential differences. While keeping your code **DRY** (which stands for **Don't Repeat Yourself**) should already be part of your workflow, the importance of creating dynamic and reproduceable data scrubbing and transformation activities actually alludes to maintaining data consistency across your organization.

The importance of accuracy and consistency

Back in *Chapter 2*, we emphasized the importance of getting intimately familiar with both the input and output data attributes. Because it is so easy to apply mathematical functions or transform data, it is incredibly easy to transform data *incorrectly*. The accuracy of data transformation techniques requires a focused study to be done to validate and interpret the data after each step of transformation activities, fueled by a strong foundation of domain knowledge about the data itself. Thus, the process of maintaining the input data's message is not simply accomplished through a strictly intuitive approach to interpretation.

As soon as you make code changes to your source data, you become a "steward of the data," which means that you now take ownership of the data produced by your cleansing and transformation tasks. Data accuracy and consistency are both pivotal to the overall success of any data pipeline, and are explained as follows:

- *Data accuracy* refers to how close your data values are to the actual or true value. For instance, if your data represents the number of sales per day, how close to true is the resulting data after moving through your ETL pipeline? If the resulting data is pretty far off, you're going to face some problems. Inaccurate data can lead to misinformed business decisions, inaccurate predictions, and ultimately, a loss of trust in the data systems. Miscalculations can lead to minor misunderstandings about the total number of customers as well as larger, more substantial errors that lead to costly overproduction and a surplus of inventory beyond the needs of a company.

- *Data consistency* ensures that data across all platforms and systems in an organization presents a unified and coherent view of the data. Consistent data enables a single source of truth, which is essential for operational efficiency and effective decision-making. For pipelines that use similar data, how consistent are the values across processes? As it is right now, data is often stored in multiple databases or systems, and inconsistency between data sources created from separate pipelines is not uncommon. This always leads to confusion within non-technical teams that use the data, as well as duplicative work and a general mistrust of the data as a whole.

This is why maintaining data accuracy and consistency and ensuring data integrity must be the core values of a data engineer when designing high-quality data pipelines. By implementing robust and reusable data validation, cleansing, and integration practices, data engineers help eliminate inaccuracies and inconsistencies. An ETL pipeline can be designed to harmonize data from multiple sources. Ultimately, data accuracy and consistency are not just about having clean data; they are about building trust in data, which leads to informed decision-making and a competitive advantage in the marketplace. The following diagram displays some common problems pertaining to data quality:

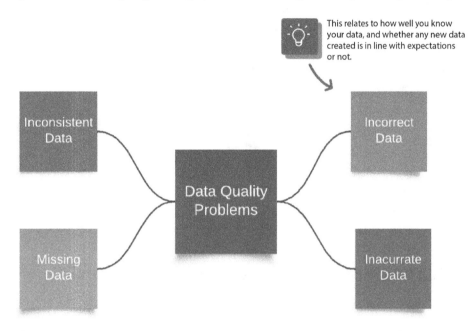

This relates to how well you know your data, and whether any new data created is in line with expectations or not.

Figure 5.1: Common data quality problems

Understanding the downstream applications of your data

Spending time and resources to ensure highly accurate data annotation is an essential step in data pipeline creation, but it's often overlooked by the engineers constructing them. Typically, the burden of data preprocessing is primarily placed on data analysts and data scientists, who are commonly the ones who use the output data downstream. However, extrapolating the "ground truth" from the source data should be approached as a shared responsibility. The identification of the factual truth available within the input data source helps inform you as the engineer what additional labels or alterations need to be made to streamline the creation of the desired output data.

The significance of different attributes within the data is predetermined by the inclusion criteria of the dataset. Data definitions impact the magnitude of the dataset's ability to inform about its subject matter as well as the incidence of "data drift," referring to changes in the meaning of data definitions due to updates to attributes in newly added data. These concepts are important to keep in mind as you identify which values make sense to transform, and which values require disaggregated representations in order to maintain their original meaning. This prevents the dreaded **garbage in, garbage out** (also known as **GIGO**), where, if you put flawed data into a pipeline, your output is flawed too.

With these principles clearly defined at the initiation of a new pipeline workflow, all modifications and future improvements to data transformation methodologies will be built to improve the pipeline's ability to effectively produce accurate output data. These methodologies are listed in *Figure 5.2*:

Transformations
• Standards (uppercase, lowercase, acronyms, and abbreviations)
• Normalization (such as, enforcing business roles)
• Corrections
• Correct null values
• Change data type
• Duplicate data resolution
• Data integrity enforcement

Figure 5.2: Methods of data transformation

Strategies for data cleansing and transformation in Python

Python's rich ecosystem of data-centric libraries, such as Pandas and NumPy, allows the seamless detection and correction of inconsistencies, errors, or missing values, leading to better data integrity and reliability. In transformation, data is reshaped, normalized, or aggregated to suit specific needs. Python's flexibility enables complex transformations and operations such as merging datasets, grouping data, or creating pivot tables, which are often necessary for advanced analytics or machine learning models.

Preliminary tasks – the importance of staging data

The extracted data is sent to a temporary storage area called the data staging area prior to the transformation and cleansing process. This is done to avoid the need to extract data again, should any problem occur (reference: *A Five-Layered Business Intelligence Architecture* by In Ong et al.).

Step 1 – data discovery and interpretation

As mentioned in the previous chapter, the inevitable usefulness of the output data is reliant on accurately representing the input data in its new transformation. All fields required in the output data need to be mapped from attributes of the input data, and each layer of data processing should be designed to perform a specific set of tasks that produce a known output data requirement. Often, multiple transformations are required to accomplish this. It helps to think about input data and transformation functions as ingredients:

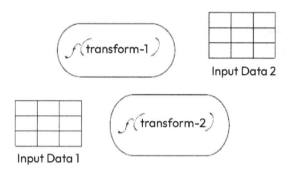

Figure 5.3: Input data and transformation functions as ingredients

Let's take the example of road crash data for the City of Chicago. The data can be found at https:// data.cityofchicago.org/, the official website of the City of Chicago. As a word of caution, the City of Chicago does not guarantee the content, accuracy, timeliness, or completeness of the data provided on this site. The data is subject to change without prior notice. Users acknowledge that they are using the data at their own risk.

In the chapter5 directory on GitHub, you'll find three data files: traffic_crashes.csv, traffic_crash_vehicle.csv, and traffic_crash_people.csv.

Let's import the traffic_crashes.csv file into a Jupyter Notebook to understand the data. There are various methods to see the full picture of input data. We will use a profiling library in conjunction with Pandas to understand the data in subsequent chapters.

We will do some basic operations to understand the data. A data engineer should look, touch, feel, and smell the data before designing an ETL pipeline. The best way to do this is by using the Jupyter Notebook.

Running the following code in the Jupyter Notebook yields the first five rows of crash data:

```
import pandas as pd
df_crashes = pd.read_csv("data/traffic_crashes.csv")
df_crashes.head()
```

The following screenshot is a representation of what the preceding code will output into your Jupyter Notebook:

```
df_crashes.head()
```

	crash_record_id	rd_no	crash_date_est_i	crash_date	posted_speed_limit	traffic_control_device	device_condition
0	530411c8611eb0ccb9b25f16b2955cd21761fa1928dcaa...	JE494048	NaN	2021-12-31T14:00:00.000	35	NO CONTROLS	NO CONTROLS
1	305b06235b250aa0029c07313c84f969f4bc13c1cc3715...	JE494008	NaN	2021-12-31T14:00:00.000	30	TRAFFIC SIGNAL	UNKNOWN
2	444221c2a9bc82fc4f301082ab22b482d7d661cf88fcdf...	JE494016	Y	2021-12-31T13:56:00.000	10	OTHER	NO CONTROLS
3	4603435fbb4ef5d45c0d805c3e9aa5558a311a140a737e...	JE494049	NaN	2021-12-31T13:46:00.000	30	NO CONTROLS	NO CONTROLS
4	db62bb4534d0dae57112ea3ff8d50193784aaa732ed58d...	JE494000	NaN	2021-12-31T13:45:00.000	30	TRAFFIC SIGNAL	FUNCTIONING PROPERLY

5 rows × 49 columns

Figure 5.4: Data output of first five rows of Chicago's traffic crash data

You should look at the first few rows to understand the data. Being familiar with how the input data is visualized by the human eye is important, especially when assessing the types of transformations available for the data type shown. For example, dates can be transformed into a weekly or monthly data column, or string-float columns can be transformed into integer-float columns with a standardized decimal. But how do you determine whether the input data is "bad" or "good"?

Step 2 – checking for missing or invalid data

Data can be quite messy, especially when dealing with new data sources. "Cleaning" the data by checking for data corruption is an important data exploration step to perform prior to manipulating the input data. The integrity of the source data needs to be systematically identified, and this is accomplished by checking for missing, invalid, or inconsistent data structures, or duplicate data entries. Data quality can be maintained by identifying the predictable "bad" data and creating a remedy within the pipeline to transform it into usable preliminary values for accurate data mapping.

Now, it's time to do the data cleansing. We can use Pandas' built-in `info()` method for this purpose:

```
df_crashes.info()
```

The `info()` method is useful for gaining a general overview of the DataFrame's structure and assessing the quality and completeness of the data. It's a quick view of the number of rows and columns, the data types of each column, and the memory usage, as well as the total non-null values in each column, which helps to identify missing data. You can see the output of the `info()` method on our crash dataset as follows:

```
df_crashes.info()

<class 'pandas.core.frame.DataFrame'>
RangeIndex: 1000 entries, 0 to 999
Data columns (total 49 columns):
 #   Column                       Non-Null Count  Dtype
---  ------                       --------------  -----
 0   crash_record_id              1000 non-null   object
 1   rd_no                        1000 non-null   object
 2   crash_date_est_i             69 non-null     object
 3   crash_date                   1000 non-null   object
 4   posted_speed_limit           1000 non-null   int64
 5   traffic_control_device       1000 non-null   object
 6   device_condition             1000 non-null   object
 7   weather_condition            1000 non-null   object
 8   lighting_condition           1000 non-null   object
 9   first_crash_type             1000 non-null   object
 10  trafficway_type              1000 non-null   object
 11  lane_cnt                     1 non-null      float64
 12  alignment                    1000 non-null   object
 13  roadway_surface_cond         1000 non-null   object
 14  road_defect                  1000 non-null   object
 15  report_type                  976 non-null    object
 16  crash_type                   1000 non-null   object
 17  intersection_related_i       271 non-null    object
 18  private_property_i           45 non-null     object
 19  hit_and_run_i                320 non-null    object
 20  damage                       1000 non-null   object
 21  date_police_notified         1000 non-null   object
 22  prim_contributory_cause      1000 non-null   object
 23  sec_contributory_cause       1000 non-null   object
 24  street_no                    1000 non-null   int64
 25  street_direction             1000 non-null   object
 26  street_name                  1000 non-null   object
 27  beat_of_occurrence           1000 non-null   int64
 28  photos_taken_i               15 non-null     object
 29  statements_taken_i           22 non-null     object
 30  dooring_i                    0 non-null      float64
 31  work_zone_i                  4 non-null      object
 32  work_zone_type               3 non-null      object
 33  workers_present_i            1 non-null      object
 34  num_units                    1000 non-null   int64
 35  most_severe_injury           998 non-null    object
 36  injuries_total               998 non-null    float64
 37  injuries_fatal               998 non-null    float64
 38  injuries_incapacitating      998 non-null    float64
 39  injuries_non_incapacitating  998 non-null    float64
 40  injuries_reported_not_evident 998 non-null   float64
 41  injuries_no_indication       998 non-null    float64
 42  injuries_unknown             998 non-null    float64
 43  crash_hour                   1000 non-null   int64
 44  crash_day_of_week            1000 non-null   int64
 45  crash_month                  1000 non-null   int64
 46  latitude                     987 non-null    float64
 47  longitude                    987 non-null    float64
 48  location                     987 non-null    object
dtypes: float64(11), int64(7), object(31)
memory usage: 382.9+ KB
```

Figure 5.5: Count of non-null values by column in Chicago's traffic crash data

This gives the non-null elements for each field. The missing data can be calculated based on this formula: *number of rows – non-null elements.*

Alternatively, `df_crashes.isnull().sum()` returns the number of missing data instances (null values) in each field:

```
df_crashes.isnull().sum()

crash_record_id                   0
rd_no                             0
crash_date_est_i                931
crash_date                        0
posted_speed_limit                0
traffic_control_device            0
device_condition                  0
weather_condition                 0
lighting_condition                0
first_crash_type                  0
trafficway_type                   0
lane_cnt                        999
alignment                         0
roadway_surface_cond              0
road_defect                       0
report_type                      24
crash_type                        0
intersection_related_i          729
private_property_i              955
hit_and_run_i                   680
damage                            0
date_police_notified              0
prim_contributory_cause           0
sec_contributory_cause            0
street_no                         0
street_direction                  0
street_name                       0
beat_of_occurrence                0
photos_taken_i                  985
statements_taken_i              978
dooring_i                      1000
work_zone_i                     996
work_zone_type                  997
workers_present_i               999
num_units                         0
most_severe_injury                2
injuries_total                    2
injuries_fatal                    2
injuries_incapacitating           2
injuries_non_incapacitating       2
injuries_reported_not_evident     2
injuries_no_indication            2
injuries_unknown                  2
crash_hour                        0
crash_day_of_week                 0
crash_month                       0
latitude                         13
longitude                        13
location                         13
dtype: int64
```

Figure 5.6: Count of null values by column in Chicago's traffic crash data

Dropping columns with all null values

There is no purpose in keeping a column where all values are missing. We can drop all such columns as follows:

```
df_crashes.dropna(axis='columns', how='all', inplace=True)
```

Dropping rows with too many missing values

To ensure data quality, it is important to exclude rows that contain no usable data; in other words, data that is inconsistent, missing, or incorrect. Before implementing a logic to drop such rows, we need to establish the criteria for determining usable elements. Let's assume that we want to remove rows with less than three usable elements. In Pandas, the `dropna()` method offers the `thresh` argument, which allows us to set the threshold for the number of usable elements, enabling us to effectively filter out unwanted rows:

```
df_crashes = df_crashes.dropna(axis='index', thresh=2,
    inplace=False)
```

The preceding statement will remove all the rows where the number of elements is less than three.

Working with missing data

As we can see from *Figure 5.6*, the `report type` column has 24 null values:

```
# This column has only two values.
df_crashes['report_type'].unique()
# ['ON SCENE', 'NOT ON SCENE (DESK REPORT)']

  # Let's fill the missing value with 'ON SCENE' as below -
  df_crashes  = df_crashes.fillna(value={'report_type': 'ON SCENE'})
```

We will learn more about numerous data manipulation methods in subsequent chapters.

Merging datasets and data aggregation

Let's see how we can merge different datasets. We have methods to do all SQL joins on datasets using Pandas. We already have the `df_crashes` dataset handy. We will read another dataset from the `traffic_crash_vehicle.csv` file. Let's read this file and create a `df_vehicles` DataFrame:

```
df_vehicles= pd.read_csv("data/traffic_crash_vehicle.csv")
```

The `df_crashes` and `df_vehicles` DataFrames have a common `crash_record_id` field. The following command performs an inner join:

```
df = df_crashes.merge(df_vehicles, how = 'left',
    on='crash_record_id',suffixes=('_left', '_right'))
```

What does this code mean, exactly? In the following diagram, you'll see how a left merge specifically works. Since the df_crashes data is on the *left side* of the .merge() function, its data is prioritized in the merge while the df_vehicles data on the *right side* is left behind. Thus, only the data from the df_vehicles DataFrame is used in the crash_record_id column:

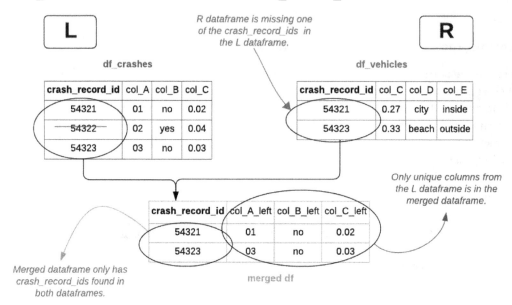

Figure 5.7: Visualization of a left-hand merge between two DataFrames

Now, it is time to perform some aggregations on the merged dataframe df. Let's look at the following facts based on the merged data.

The total number of passenger cars involved in the crash can be found using the following code:

```
df.groupby('vehicle_type').agg({'crash_record_id':
    'count'}).reset_index()
```

As we can see from the following screenshot, the number of passenger vehicles involved in a crash is 633:

	vehicle_type	crash_record_id
0	BUS OVER 15 PASS.	5
1	MOPED OR MOTORIZED BICYCLE	1
2	OTHER	20
3	OTHER VEHICLE WITH TRAILER	1
4	PASSENGER	633
5	PICKUP	33
6	SINGLE UNIT TRUCK WITH TRAILER	2
7	SPORT UTILITY VEHICLE (SUV)	138
8	TRACTOR W/ SEMI-TRAILER	5
9	TRACTOR W/O SEMI-TRAILER	2
10	TRUCK - SINGLE UNIT	14
11	UNKNOWN/NA	89
12	VAN/MINI-VAN	38

Figure 5.8: Number of crash incidents grouped by vehicle type

We can also use the following code to get the answer programmatically:

```
number_of_passenger_cars_involved = df_agg[df_agg['vehicle_type'] ==
'PASSENGER']['crash_record_id'].array[0]
```

Step 3 – data mapping with target data

Data mapping is considered an important transformation step. For each data conversion identified in *Step 1*, a methodology is written to accomplish that task. When writing the methodology of transformation, it's also important to consider the occurrence of data loss within each step, and whether the level of data loss can be mitigated by using other methods.

There is a field called vehicle_types_types in the df_vehicles DataFrame. Let's say we have an RDBMS table named Vehicle in DataWarehouse. We need to load the df_vehicle data into the Vehicle table. The vehicle_types field is loaded as vehicletype in the Vehicle table.

In other words, we need to map the vehicle_types field to vehicletypes. We create mappings using imported Excel database tables or JSON files to define the schema in a dictionary format. However, for simplicity, we will create a mapping using a Python dictionary for this example:

```
vehicle_mapping = {'vehicle_type' :  'vehicletypes'}
```

Now, it's time to apply this mapping to the merged `df` dataframe:

```
df = df.rename(columns= vehicle_mapping)
```

Let's verify the DataFrame for the `vehicletypes` column:

Renaming Data for Output

```
vehicle_mapping = {'vehicle_type':'vehicletypes'}
df_agg = df_agg.rename(columns=vehicle_mapping)
```

df_agg

	vehicletypes	crash_record_id
0	BUS OVER 15 PASS.	5
1	MOPED OR MOTORIZED BICYCLE	1
2	OTHER	20
3	OTHER VEHICLE WITH TRAILER	1
4	PASSENGER	633
5	PICKUP	33
6	SINGLE UNIT TRUCK WITH TRAILER	2
7	SPORT UTILITY VEHICLE (SUV)	138
8	TRACTOR W/ SEMI-TRAILER	5
9	TRACTOR W/O SEMI-TRAILER	2
10	TRUCK - SINGLE UNIT	14
11	UNKNOWN/NA	89
12	VAN/MINI-VAN	38

Figure 5.9: Map of vehicle types in Chicago crash data

In this section, we walked through a step-by-step process of how to approach input data and functions as the "ingredient" of your data pipeline. As of now, we know the code we want to use for each step, as we have verified that the output data is indeed in the correct format. Now, we need to apply the DRY principle to our code for use in reusable functions.

Step 4 – creating the transformation activity

Once the methodology for the data transformation has been established with sample data, the code can be rewritten to fit within a transformation activity. An activity is a term used to describe a reusable series of functions that collectively accomplish a specific transformation task. At this stage, the activity can be used to establish the anticipated computational and financial burden of a given transformation.

In your Jupyter Notebook, spend some time looking over the `get_transformed_data()` function, where we put each of the steps performed in *Step 3* into one reusable function. Once you get a feel for the code, take another look. What processes do you think are reusable? Can you break down any of the steps into separate subfunctions?

Creating a dynamic pipeline environment isn't just about putting all pipeline steps into one function. In the following section, we will walk through one method of how we can break down our pipeline steps into separate functions that can be repurposed in different pipelines, or, at a minimum, separate each step into its own action.

Step 5 – running the workflow

The workflow is the summation of all necessary transformation activities required for the final output data. In most cases, the output of the proceeding transformation serves as the input of the consecutive transformation, so this is where a smooth flow through activities needs to be established, in addition to identifying the full computational and financial burden of the transformation workflow within the pipeline.

In your Jupyter Notebook, take a look at how we broke down the `get_transformed_data()` function into a series of subfunctions:

1. Read data from data source: `read_datasources(source_name)` is a function that imports CSV data files into Pandas DataFrames.

   Drop rows with null values: `drop_rows_with_null_values(df)` is a function that drops null values based on the "set standard" (i.e., our workflow from *Step 3*).

   Fill missing values: `fill_missing_values(df)` is one function to fill in missing values based on the "set standard" (i.e., our workflow from *Step 3*).

2. Merge DataFrames: `merge_dataframes(df_vehicles,df_crashes)` is a function that merges two DataFrames.

   Note that this can be additionally modified to take in the parameters for the merge (such as how, on, and `suffixes`), but we will leave this out for simplicity's sake.

3. Rename columns: `rename_columns(df)` is a function that renames columns.

   Note that this can also be modified to be more dynamic by making parameters for the columns to be renamed.

Step 6 – post-transformation check

With all the transformation activities cleanly strung into a defined workflow, the quality of the resulting output data must be confirmed. This means carefully looking for missing records, new errors introduced during the transformation workflow, and any other form of irregular data inconsistencies that undermine the integrity of the output data. We will look into various ways to perform the post-transformation check in subsequent chapters.

Transformation activities in Python

When designing the first iterations of data manipulation activity in a pipeline, it's best to start off with a chunk of sample data as opposed to processing the entire data source. This way, you can start to develop your workflow using 1,000 rows of data instead of 10,000 in order to save on both GPUs and development time.

To do this at a high level, let's add some logging and error handling around our functions from the previous section. Don't worry too much about the type of logging for now. We will go more into this later on in *Chapter 14.*

We will now describe how we can utilize the functions created in the previous section as the foundation for individual transformation activities:

1. Create `read_data_pipeline(crash_file, vehicle_file)` to use `read_datasources(source_name)` to import the crash and vehicle files into individual DataFrames.

2. Use `drop_rows_with_null_values_pipeline(df_crash, df_vehicle)` to use `drop_rows_with_null_values(df)` on both the crash and vehicle DataFrames.

3. Use `fill_missing_values_pipeline(df_crash, df_vehicle)` to fill missing values in the crash and vehicle DataFrames with `fill_missing_values(df)`.

4. Merge the crash and vehicle DataFrames using `merge_dataframes_pipeline(df_crash, df_vehicle)` to run the `merge_dataframes(df_vehicles, df_crashes)` function.

5. Lastly, use `format_dataframes_pipeline(df_agg)` to run `rename_columns(df)` to rename columns.

Finally, in the next section, we put it all together into a single pipeline workflow function.

Creating data pipeline activity in Python

The following code shows how we can convert the `get_transformed_data()` function to a Python workflow:

```
def get_transformed_data(crash_file, vehicle_file):
    # Read Data Pipeline
    df_crash, df_vehicle = read_data_pipeline(crash_file,
    vehicle_file)

    # Drop Nulls
    df_crash, df_vehicle = drop_rows_with_null_values_pipeline(df_
crash, df_vehicle)

    # Fill in Missing Values
    df_crash, df_vehicle = fill_missing_values_pipeline(df_crash, df_
vehicle)
```

```
# Merge Dataframes
df_agg = merge_dataframes_pipeline(df_crash, df_vehicle)

# Reformat for Output
df_output = format_dataframes_pipeline(df_agg)
return df_output
```

Now that we have discussed the strategies, let's summarize what we've learned.

Summary

The data cleansing and transformation steps within a data pipeline are fundamental processes that are central to preparing high-quality output datasets. Creating a systematic approach to identifying and rectifying inconsistencies, inaccuracies, and missing values enhances data integrity and reliability while refining and tailoring the data to match the specific needs of your end user. Your output data can then be confidently used for any data-driven decision-making, analysis, and machine learning.

As data continues to grow in size and complexity, mastering data cleansing and transformation techniques becomes increasingly crucial, enabling data-driven organizations to uncover hidden insights and streamline operations. It is a ubiquitous and valuable skill in today's data-dependent world.

In the next chapter, we will discuss how to load transformed data into tables.

6

Loading Transformed Data

After data has undergone processing and transformation within an ETL pipeline, the final step involves transferring it to its designated final location. The type of output location that's used is determined by both the data's specific utility and the tools available within your environment.

It is most common to store output data iterations within structured, relational databases. Such databases offer an easily accessible format conducive to both analytical exploration and forthcoming modifications.

In this chapter, we'll get more acquainted with the "L" of ETL pipelines and the best practices for designing efficient load operations. We will discuss how to optimize load activities to fit the output data using either incremental or full data loading activities. Finally, we'll provide a comprehensive walkthrough for creating a **relational database management system (RDBMS)** on your local device that you can utilize as the output location for our data for the remainder of this book.

This chapter will proceed as follows:

- Introduction to data loading
- Best practices for data loading
- Optimizing data load activities by controlling the data import method
- Precautions to consider
- Tutorial – preparing your local environment for data loading activities

Technical requirements

To effectively utilize the resources and code examples provided in this chapter, ensure that your system meets the following technical requirements:

- Software requirements:

  - **Integrated development environment** (IDE): We recommend using PyCharm as the preferred IDE for working with Python, and we might make specific references to PyCharm throughout this chapter. However, you are free to use any Python-compatible IDE of your choice.

- Jupyter Notebooks should be installed.

- Python version 3.6 or higher should be installed.

- Pipenv should be installed to manage dependencies.

- GitHub repository: The associated code and resources for this chapter can be found in this book's GitHub repository at `https://github.com/PacktPublishing/Building-ETL-Pipelines-with-Python`. Fork and clone the repository to your local machine.

Introduction to data loading

Data loading is the final step of the ETL process, and arguably the entire purpose of the data pipeline. The loading phase of your ETL process requires careful preparation to ensure the transformed data is seamlessly transitioned to its destination.

Choosing the load destination

The choice of destination greatly impacts data accessibility, storage, querying capabilities, and overall system performance. Depending on the nature of your project, you might be loading data into relational databases, cloud-based data warehouses, NoSQL stores, or other repositories. Understanding the target system's requirements and capabilities is a foundational step to designing an efficient loading strategy. Consider factors such as data types, indexing, partitioning, and data distribution.

Python's adaptability ensures that, regardless of your destination choice, you have the tools at hand to integrate, manipulate, and optimize data loading processes effectively.

Types of load destinations

Python offers a versatile ecosystem of libraries and tools that seamlessly interface with various load destinations.

Relational databases

Relational databases remain the most common locations for data storage and management. Python provides support for popular RDBMSs such as MySQL, PostgreSQL, SQLite, and Oracle. Utilizing libraries such as `SQLAlchemy` and database-specific drivers (for example, `psycopg2` and `pymysql`) allows you to efficiently load data into structured tables. These databases offer the advantage of data integrity enforcement, transaction management, and support for complex querying.

Later in this chapter, we will walk you through how to create a local PostgreSQL database on your device. We will use that database as the data load destination for many examples throughout this book.

Data warehouses

Data warehouses are primarily used for storing large data for long-term storage; they have gained popularity over the years as scalable repositories optimized for complex analytical queries and reporting. While the creation, management, and overhead of a data warehouse goes beyond the scope of this book, Python has a plethora of libraries, such as Pandas, and specialized connectors to efficiently load data into data warehouses such as Amazon Redshift, Google BigQuery, and Snowflake.

NoSQL stores

For semi-structured and unstructured data, NoSQL databases such as MongoDB, Cassandra, and Couchbase provide flexible and schemaless data storage. Python tools such as `pymongo` and `cassandra-driver` enable seamless integration with these databases. NoSQL stores are well-suited for scenarios that require high scalability, rapid data ingestion, and unstructured data types.

Later in this chapter, we will walk you through how to create a local Cassandra database on your device, and how to use it as a data load destination.

Filesystems and object storage

Filesystems and object storage (for example, Amazon S3 and Azure Blob Storage) are also advantageous for archiving, making backups, and scenarios where direct database integration is not required. Python's built-in I/O capabilities and third-party libraries simplify the process of writing data to files or cloud-based storage.

In *Chapter 9*, we will introduce using **Amazon Web Services** (**AWS**) S3 while you're propagating your data pipeline.

Best practices for data loading

There isn't one universally definitive approach to creating data pipeline loading activities, but some methods are *more effective* than others. Proper preparation and adherence to best practices empower you to navigate the data loading phase with confidence, optimizing efficiency, accuracy, and reliability in your ETL workflow.

The process of designing a data loading activity reflects the level of understanding you have of the full environmental conditions of your system. You can use the following three principles to design a data loading workflow that is both scalable and reusable:

- Utilizing techniques such as bulk loading, parallel processing, and optimized SQL queries can significantly enhance loading performance for large datasets. By adopting scalable strategies, you ensure that your data loading solution remains efficient and responsive even as data volume increases.

- Automation streamlines the loading process, reducing the risk of human errors and enhancing consistency. Implementing automated loading routines using Python scripts or ETL tools facilitates scheduled or event-driven data loading.

- Proactive monitoring empowers you to identify and rectify issues promptly, contributing to data integrity and system reliability. Incorporating robust logging enables you to track loading activities, performance metrics, and potential errors.

Now that you are aware of the best practices, let's dive into our next topic of optimizing data loads.

Optimizing data loading activities by controlling the data import method

From the aforementioned list, this chapter specifically focuses on utilizing different loading strategies to design efficient loading activities. Later in this book, we will dive deeper into automation Python modules and cloud resources (*Chapters 8* and *9*), and monitoring ETL pipelines (*Chapter 14*). But for now, let's focus on the two most common methods for data loads: full and incremental.

Creating demo data

We will utilize Python's `sqlite3` database to walk through a demo of how full and incremental data loads can be formed using Python. From the `chapter_06/` directory in your PyCharm environment, open the `Loading_Transformed_Data.ipynb` file by initiating Jupyter in your PyCharm terminal by running the following command:

```
(venv) (base) usr@usr-MBP chapter_06  % jupyter notebook
```

Verify that the following code is in your Jupyter notebook:

```python
# import modules
import sqlite3

# demo data
laundry_mat_data = [
    {"product": "Detergent", "dollar_price_per_unit": 4.5,
        "quantity": 100, "total_cost": 200},
    {"product": "Dryer Sheets Box",
        "dollar_price_per_unit": 3.5, "quantity": 100,
        "total_cost": 350},
    {"product": "Washing Machine",
        "dollar_price_per_unit": 400, "quantity": 25,
        "total_cost": 10000},
    {"product": "Dryer", "dollar_price_per_unit": 400,
        "quantity": 25, "total_cost": 10000},
]
```

Create a connection instance, `conn`, and a connection cursor, `cursor`, and add them to a new sqlite database named `laundry_mat`:

```
# Connect to the database
conn = sqlite3.connect("laundry_mat.db")
cursor = conn.cursor()
```

Full data loads

In theory, data pipeline design intends to load the output data in one pass. This is desirable because it closes the process of the one clean sweep, smoothly transferring data from one location to another, and providing the opportunity for review and improvement before the next iteration of the cycle.

If we were to load `laundry_mat_data` into a `laundry_mat` database using a full data load method, first, we must truncate any existing data:

```
cursor.execute("DELETE FROM laundry_mat")
```

Then, for each record row in `laundry_mat_data`, we must insert the new data into `laundry_mat` using an `INSERT INTO laundry_mat` statement:

```
for record in laundry_mat_data:
        cursor.execute("INSERT INTO laundry_mat (product,
                dollar_price_per_unit, quantity,
                total_cost) VALUES (?, ?, ?, ?)",
                    (record["product"],
                    Record["dollar_price_per_unit"],
                    Record["quantity"],
                    record["total_cost"]))
```

However, in many situations, a full data load might not be a viable option. These situations include client requirements for continuous access to the full dataset or working with daily updates for incredibly large and complex datasets, such as financial data. In these types of situations, taking an incremental approach is advisable.

Incremental data loads

Incremental data loads are a viable option for breaking up the computational impact of large data loads into an output data location by processing loading activities in smaller, more manageable chunks.

A word of caution: incremental data loads also require a healthy amount of error-handling procedures, especially when you're trying to maintain sequential data. Incremental processes need to be able to manage incomplete data loads as well as handle duplicate data imports. The cadence of data creation as well as incremental data loads need to be in sync before you commit an incremental data load approach.

When using `laundry_mat_data` to perform incremental data loads, we don't need to truncate the table before importing new data. Instead of populating the `laundry_mat` database using a full data load method, we can use an `INSERT OR IGNORE INTO laundry_mat` statement to insert new data, as well as ignore duplicate records:

```
for record in laundry_mat_data:
        cursor.execute("INSERT OR IGNORE INTO laundry_mat
                (product, dollar_price_per_unit, quantity,
                total_cost) VALUES (?, ?, ?, ?)",
                    (record["product"],
                    Record["dollar_price_per_unit"],
                    Record["quantity"],
                    record["total_cost"]))
```

Now that we have a better understanding of how we can control data loading activities by using full or incremental import methods, let's look at some of the technical challenges you may face when creating effective data load activities.

Precautions to consider

Back in *Chapter 2*, we referenced that there is a wide range of purposes for data pipelines, ranging from daily updates for business analytics dashboards to cyclical long-term storage. Since many organizations make decisions based on the resulting output data, not only is the accuracy of data transformations crucial, but the resulting format and quality of the data loaded need to remain cohesive with the data that already exists within the target location.

In a clean, reproducible, and scalable data ecosystem, the target data output location maintains its own, arguably authoritative, structure that serves as the ground truth for business data within your company. It requires you to scrutinously manage the ongoing ETL processes that keep the storage environment up to date. When discussing the differences between full and incremental data loads in the previous section, it became clear that there is a need to distinguish between new, freshly curated data and existing, sometimes legacy, data during loading.

The most effective approach appears to be leveraging batch loading tools inherent in many RDBMSs as they circumvent these issues. Other techniques include creating custom indexing based on data rules within your database as well as maximizing the utilization of CPU resources. Collectively, these strategies contribute to a smoother and more efficient loading process, enhancing the overall effectiveness of data warehouse management.

Next, we'll switch gears and focus on the types of data storage locations we have available since the `sqlite3` database that we used earlier in this chapter is rarely used in deployable data pipelines. In the following section, we will walk you through how to create a PostgreSQL database on your device so that you can use it as an output location for our load activities throughout the rest of this book.

Tutorial – preparing your local environment for data loading activities

In this section, we will use a local PostgreSQL database as the data load destination; we will do the same for many of the examples throughout this book. PostgreSQL is a free and open source RDBMS and supports SQL compliance. You can learn more about PostgreSQL at `https://en.wikipedia.org/wiki/PostgreSQL`.

Downloading and installing PostgreSQL

Depending on your device, select the respective download link in your browser (`https://www.enterprisedb.com/downloads/postgres-postgresql-downloads`) and follow these steps:

1. Download the **postgres.app** installer.

2. Click on the `.dmg` file and double-click the box to initiate the download.

3. Once the files are downloaded, the EDB PostgreSQL Setup Wizard will begin. Make sure you choose the following criteria during your installation:

Installation Directory	`/Library/PostgreSQL/15`
Port	`5432`
Select Components	• PostgreSQL Server • pgAdmin 4 • Stack Builder • Command Line Tools
Data Directory	`/Library/PostgreSQL/15/data`
Password	\<insert your master password\>
Advanced Options	[Default locale]
Stack Builder	\<unselect open on close\>

Table 6.1: Installation criteria

Open the **pgAdmin** application on your local device and enter the password you created in the PostgreSQL Setup Wizard:

Figure 6.1: Screenshot of where PostgreSQL displays your master password input

4.   In the **Quick Links** section of the home page, select **Add New Server**:

Name	Packt_ETL
Host	localhost
Port	5432
User	postgre
Database	chicago_dmv
Password	<insert your master password>
Connection URL	postgresql://localhost

Table 6.2: Server details

Creating data schemas in PostgreSQL

With our PostgreSQL environment and database officially initiated, it's time to add some data. Since we are treating the chicago_dmv database as our output data location, we want to create a data schema, also known as a data expectation, for the columns and required data types of any data stored within a given data table.

Just as with data tables, the name of a data schema must be unique within the database. We will use the same naming convention that we used for the database to name the data schema – that is, `chicago_schema`. To create `chicago_schema`, click on the database, select **Create | Schema**, and enter your chosen schema name in the `ChicagoName` slot. We want to create a schema with the following requirements:

Name	Data Type	Can be NULL	Primary Key	Default Value
primaryID	int	No	Yes	01
num_column	bitint	Yes	-	6749380428
string_column	char	Yes	-	"this is a string"
json_column	json	Yes	-	{ "key": 1 }

Table 6.3: New schema details

Enter this information into the **Create | Schema** GUI and click **Save**.

These data requirements are simplistic but helpful. Each column has an expected data type, which means that any data that is inserted into this table must have the same column names and data types; otherwise, the data import process will fail. By predefining the data requirements of your output data location with a data schema, you ensure that the pipeline was indeed built to fulfill all the requirements for the pipeline in the first place. Leveraging table schemas is an excellent way to instill data integrity practices.

Summary

In this chapter, we introduced the premise of ETL pipeline data loading activities, as well as some of the contingencies of designing these activities correctly. We walked through the essential steps of setting up data storage destinations and structuring schemas in anticipation of the resultant data from our pipeline. We also introduced a blend of Python capabilities to fully or incrementally load data using SQLite. Lastly, we set up our local environment with PostgreSQL, which we will use as our data loading output location for the remainder of this book. In the next chapter, we will guide you through the entire process of creating a fully operational data pipeline.

7

Tutorial – Building an End-to-End ETL Pipeline in Python

Python is a programming language with a rich ecosystem of libraries and tools, which results in it being an excellent platform for building robust, reliable, and flexible ETL pipelines. So far in this book, we have taken a granular, piecewise look at each step of the ETL process in pure Python.

In this chapter, we'll walk through a practical, comprehensive approach to creating a full end-to-end ETL pipeline using Python-related tools. By the end of this chapter, you will be able to extract data, perform necessary cleansing and transformation activities, and load the processed data into a PostgreSQL database table.

In this chapter, you will accomplish the following tasks:

- **Data extraction**: Read the source CSV files and store the data in separate DataFrames
- **Data cleansing and transformation**: Perform key data cleaning and transformation activities on each DataFrame to prepare the data so that it can be imported to the desired output location:

  - Remove duplicate rows

  - Handle missing values

  - Convert columns into their appropriate data types

  - Merge the DataFrames into a single DataFrame

  - Drop unnecessary columns

  - Rename columns so that they match the output data schema

- **Data loading**: Load the data from the merged DataFrame into PostgreSQL tables:

  - Create a PostgreSQL database

  - Create PostgreSQL data tables based on table schemas

- Use the `psycopg2` module to connect to the PostgreSQL database
- Execute SQL queries to create the table and insert data into the PostgreSQL database

By accomplishing these tasks, you will be able to extract, transform, and load the data from the CSV files into a PostgreSQL database table.

Technical requirements

We encourage you to keep the previous chapters on standby for easy reference as we work through the tutorial of what a work situation might require you to do. To effectively utilize the resources and code examples provided in this chapter, ensure that your system meets the following technical requirements:

- Software requirements:
    - **Integrated development environment** (**IDE**): We recommend using **PyCharm** as the preferred IDE for working with Python, and we might make specific references to PyCharm throughout this chapter. However, you are free to use any Python-compatible IDE of your choice.
    - Jupyter Notebooks should be installed.
    - Python version 3.6 or higher should be installed.
    - Pipenv should be installed for managing dependencies.
- GitHub repository: The associated code and resources for this chapter can be found in this book's GitHub repository at `https://github.com/PacktPublishing/Building-ETL-Pipelines-with-Python`. Fork and clone the repository to your local machine.

Introducing the project

Imagine that your engineering firm is hired by a data science start-up – SafeRoad, a cutting-edge start-up – to create a custom data pipeline that seamlessly connects to the city of Chicago's open data portal. SafeRoad intends to analyze Chicago's vehicle crash data and is particularly interested in uncovering the factors responsible for these incidents.

The approach

To accomplish SafeRoad's data request, your supervisor suggests modeling the data with a PostgreSQL database. As you may recall, PostgreSQL stands tall as a robust and open source **relational database management system** (**RDBMS**). PostgreSQL is a strong database choice since it's not only cost-effective but it can also be utilized to build an ETL pipeline to easily load the database tables using pure Python. Your supervisor also mentions that the PostgreSQL database schema can be used to optimize queries to safeguard against pipeline crashes. You take note of their suggestions, then start acquainting yourselves with the data:

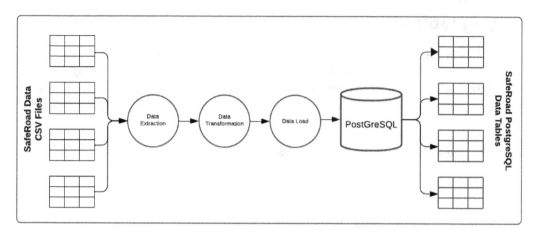

Figure 7.1: Simple pipeline diagram of the approach

The data

In light of the Chicago open data portal's vast collection of data schemas, SafeRoad's Data Science team has provided the requested data schema for the following tables:

- Vehicle
- Person
- Time
- Crash

Taking a look at the data, each table within the source dataset adheres to a tabular structure, indicating a well-organized and structured data format. This reaffirms your supervisor's suggestion to use PostgreSQL since this storage system requires structured data sources. You decide to take a look at the data. In the GitHub repository, in the chapter_07/data directory, head to the schema. md file, where you will find the schema descriptions for each source data table. Spend some time getting familiar with the column names, column data types, and example data values for the Crash, Vehicle, Time, and Person datasets. We will be creating these schemas within a PostgreSQL database in the next section.

Creating tables in PostgreSQL

Creating tables in PostgreSQL is a fundamental aspect of the database design and ease management for your client. In general, data tables serve as the foundation for structuring and storing data in a relational database management system such as PostgreSQL. By carefully designing tables, we can define the structure, relationships, and constraints that govern how data is stored and accessed. Let's take a look:

1. Open your terminal and connect to the PostgreSQL server (that you installed in the previous chapter) by running the following command:

    ```
    psql -U postgres
    ```

2. Create a new database called `chicago_vehicle_crash_data`:

    ```
    CREATE DATABASE chicago_vehicle_crash_data;
    ```

3. Create a new data schema, `chicago_dmv`, within the `chicago_vehicle_crash_data` database:

    ```
    CREATE SCHEMA chicago_dmv;
    ```

4. Verify that the new schema has been created by running the following command:

    ```
    \dn
    ```

5. Create a new data table for the `Vehicle` dataset using the `chicago_dmv` schema:

    ```
    CREATE TABLE chicago_dmv.Vehicle (
                    CRASH_UNIT_ID integer,
                    CRASH_ID text,
                    CRASH_DATE timestamp,
                    VEHICLE_ID integer,
                    VEHICLE_MAKE text,
                    VEHICLE_MODEL. Text,
                    VEHICLE_YEAR integer
                    VEHICLE_TYPE text
                    );
    ```

6. Using the `chicago_dmv` schema, create tables for each of the desired datasets:

- The `Person` dataset:

```
CREATE TABLE chicago_dmv.Person (
                    PERSON_ID text,
                    CRASH_ID text,
                    CRASH_DATE timestamp,
                    PERSON_TYPE text,
                    VEHICLE_ID integer,
                    PERSON_SEX text,
                    PERSON_AGE integer
                    );
```

- The `Time` dataset:

```
CREATE TABLE chicago_dmv.Time (
                    CRASH_DATE timestamp,
                    CRASH_ID text,
                    CRASH_HOUR integer,
                    CRASH_DAY_OF_WEEK integer,
                    CRASH_MONTH integer,
                    DATE_POLICE_NOTIFIED timestamp
                    );
```

- The `Crash` dataset:

```
CREATE TABLE chicago_dmv.Crash (
                    CRASH_UNIT_ID integer,
                    CRASH_ID text,
                    PERSON_ID text,
                    VEHICLE_ID integer,
                    NUM_UNITS numeric,
                    TOTAL_INJURIES numeric
                    );
```

7. Verify that the tables have been created by running the following command:

```
\dt chicago_dmv.*
```

You'll get the following output:

```
[chicago_vehicle_crash_data=# \dt chicago_dmv.*
                List of relations
     Schema    |  Name   | Type  |  Owner
--------------+---------+-------+----------
 chicago_dmv  | crash   | table | postgres
 chicago_dmv  | person  | table | postgres
 chicago_dmv  | time    | table | postgres
 chicago_dmv  | vehicle | table | postgres
(4 rows)
```

Figure 7.2: All the tables are now in the chicago_dmv schema

Congratulations on successfully creating the necessary tables in PostgreSQL! By establishing a pristine data sink with clear data definitions, you and your colleague are now ready to transition to the root purpose of this project: building a data pipeline. In the next section, we will walk you through how to create a pipeline that seamlessly populates these tables with data extracted from the original CSV files.

Sourcing and extracting the data

Back in *Chapter 5*, you might recall that we used three CSV files, `traffic_crashes.csv`, `traffic_crash_vehicle.csv`, and `traffic_crash_people.csv`, from Chicago's open data portal. Since these are the same type of files relevant to this tutorial, you can use these same data files for this section.

From your PyCharm environment, initiate your Pipenv environment from the PyCharm terminal and open a new Jupyter notebook.

Within the first cell of the notebook, type `import pandas`. Then, write the following code to read in each of the CSV files as individual DataFrames by using the Pandas `pd.read_csv()` function:

```
import pandas as pd

try:
    # Read the traffic crashes CSV file and store it in a dataframe
    df_crashes = pd.read_csv("data/traffic_crashes.csv")

    # Read the traffic crash vehicle CSV file and store it in a
dataframe
    df_vehicles = pd.read_csv("data/traffic_crash_vehicle.csv")
```

```
    # Read the traffic crash People CSV file and store it in a
dataframe
    df_people= pd.read_csv("data/traffic_crash_people.csv")

except FileNotFoundError as e:
    # Handle exception if any of the files are missing
    print(f"Error: {e}")

except Exception as e:
    # Handle any other exceptions
    print(f"Error: {e}")
```

With the data loaded into your notebook, you can start performing cleansing and transformation tasks on the data in preparation for the output data tables in PostgreSQL.

Transformation and data cleansing

As the next step in the pipeline creation tutorial, it is crucial to perform data cleansing tasks on each of the DataFrames to create reliable and trustworthy data for your clients. These tasks are essential for ensuring data quality and reliability. As a team, you decide to perform the following data cleansing tasks on each of the DataFrames:

1. **Remove duplicates**: Remove any duplicate rows in each DataFrame, if any, using the `drop_duplicates()` function:

    ```
    df = df.drop_duplicates()
    ```

2. **Handle missing values**: Check for any missing values in the DataFrames and handle them appropriately. For example, you can replace missing values in numeric columns with the mean and categorical columns with the mode using the `fillna()` function:

    ```
    # Replace missing values in numeric columns with the mean
    df.fillna(df.mean(), inplace=True)

    # Replace missing values in categorical columns with the mode
    df.fillna(df.mode().iloc[0], inplace=True)
    ```

3. **Convert data types**: Convert columns into their appropriate data types for further processing using the `astype()` function:

    ```
    # Convert columns to appropriate data types
    df['CRASH_DATE'] = pd.to_datetime(df['CRASH_DATE'],
        format='%m/%d/%Y')
    df['POSTED_SPEED_LIMIT'] = df['POSTED_SPEED_LIMIT'].
    astype('int32')
    ```

4. **Merge DataFrames**: Merge the three DataFrames into a single DataFrame based on the common columns using the `merge()` function:

```
# Merge the three dataframes into a single dataframe
merge_01_df = pd.merge(df, df2, on='CRASH_RECORD_ID')
all_data_df = pd.merge(merge_01_df, df3, on='CRASH_RECORD_ID')
```

- **Drop unnecessary columns**: Remove any unnecessary columns that are not required for further analysis using the `drop()` function:

```
# Drop unnecessary columns
df = df[['CRASH_UNIT_ID', 'CRASH_ID', 'CRASH_DATE',
    'VEHICLE_ID', 'VEHICLE_MAKE', 'VEHICLE_MODEL',
    'VEHICLE_YEAR', 'VEHICLE_TYPE', 'PERSON_ID',
    'PERSON_TYPE', 'PERSON_SEX', 'PERSON_AGE',
    'CRASH_HOUR', 'CRASH_DAY_OF_WEEK', 'CRASH_MONTH',
    'DATE_POLICE_NOTIFIED']]
```

With that, you tidied up the data by removing any duplicates in each DataFrame using the `drop_duplicates()` function, then checked for missing values and handled them by replacing missing values in numeric columns with the mean and in categorical columns with the mode using the `fillna()` function. Then, you converted the columns into their appropriate data types for further processing using the `astype()` function. After that, you merged the three DataFrames into a single DataFrame based on the common columns using the `merge()` function. Finally, you removed any unnecessary columns that were not required for further analysis using the `drop()` function.

Loading data into PostgreSQL tables

To complete the data pipeline, you need to load the transformed data into the final output locations – the PostgreSQL data tables – so that your client can easily access and use them. In this section, you will load the cleaned data into the PostgreSQL `chicago_dmv` schema using the `psycopg2` Python module. As you may recall from the previous chapter, `psycopg2` is a Python package that enables you to connect your Python (or Jupyter Notebook) script to PostgreSQL. Use the following code to establish a connection to the database from your Jupyter Notebook:

```
import psycopg2

# Establish connection to the Postgresql database
conn = psycopg2.connect(database="your_database_name",
    user="your_username", password="your_password",
    host="your_host", port="your_port")

# Create a cursor object
cur = conn.cursor()
```

Using SQL statements in Python, denoted with the beginning and end ''' quotations, you need to write insert criteria for specific values within your merged DataFrame so that they can be written to specific output locations:

- `chicago_dmv.Vehicle`:

```
insert_query_vehicle = '''INSERT INTO chicago_dmv.Vehicle
(CRASH_UNIT_ID,
CRASH_ID,
CRASH_DATE,
VEHICLE_ID,
VEHICLE_MAKE,
VEHICLE_MODEL,
VEHICLE_YEAR,
VEHICLE_TYPE)
VALUES (%s, %s, %s, %s, %s, %s, %s, %s);'''
```

- `chicago_dmv.Person`:

```
insert_query_person = '''INSERT INTO chicago_dmv.Person (PERSON_
ID,
CRASH_ID,
CRASH_DATE,
PERSON_TYPE,
VEHICLE_ID,
PERSON_SEX,
PERSON_AGE)
VALUES (%s, %s, %s, %s, %s, %s, %s);'''
```

- `chicago_dmv.Crash`:

```
insert_query_crash = '''INSERT INTO chicago_dmv.Crash (CRASH_
UNIT_ID,
CRASH_ID,
PERSON_ID,
VEHICLE_ID,
NUM_UNITS,
TOTAL_INJURIES)
VALUES (%s, %s, %s, %s, %s, %s);'''
```

With the SQL insert criteria defined, you must now loop through the merged DataFrame to get each row of the desired data and insert it into its respective database table:

```
for index, row in df.iterrows():

        # vehicles
```

```
            values_vehicle = (row['CRASH_UNIT_ID'],
                                row['CRASH_ID'],
                                 row['CRASH_DATE'],
                               row['VEHICLE_ID'],
                               row['VEHICLE_MAKE'],
                               row['VEHICLE_MODEL'],
                               row['VEHICLE_YEAR'],
                               row['VEHICLE_TYPE'])
        # Insert data int
        cur.execute(insert_query_vehicle, values_vehicle)
```

You must repeat the same process for each table and then commit the changes to the server. As a best practice, immediately close the connection to the database:

```
# Commit the changes to the database
conn.commit()
# Close the cursor and database connection
cur.close()
conn.close()
```

Making it deployable

With the workflow thoroughly tested and established within your Jupyter Notebook, the next step is to enhance the code's modularity. You can achieve this by organizing the code into separate scripts for extraction, transformation, and loading activities. By adopting a structured approach, you can ensure better maintainability and scalability of the ETL pipeline.

Design the following directory structure to create your deployable ETL pipeline:

```
project
├── data
│   ├── traffic_crashes.csv
│   ├── traffic_crash_vehicle.csv
│   └── traffic_crash_people.csv
├── etl
│   ├── __init__.py
│   ├── extract.py
│   ├── transform.py
│   └── load.py
└── config.yaml
├── main.py
├── README.md
```

In this directory structure, you have three directories – data, etl, and config:

- The data directory contains the three source data CSV files
- The etl directory contains the Python modules for each activity:

  - extract.py
  - transform.py
  - load.py
  - You also have an __init__.py file to indicate that this is a package

- The config directory contains a configuration file called database.ini that stores the database connection information

The main.py file acts as the entry point for executing the ETL pipeline and coordinates the workflow by calling the respective scripts. Additionally, there's a README.md file that provides documentation and instructions for using the ETL pipeline.

By adopting this organized directory structure, you can ensure a modular and deployable ETL pipeline that promotes code reusability, maintainability, and collaboration among team members.

Summary

This chapter provided a practical walkthrough of what it is like to be presented with a data movement problem, and the types of questions to ask as you identify which tools and resources are most suitable for your environment and your desired source data structure.

The development of an ETL workflow for SafeGuard emphasized the value of refactoring your code to become more modular, and therefore, more maintainable long-term.

In the next chapter, we will explore powerful ETL modules in Python that we can use to enhance data pipelines, and how leveraging Python modules can make our pipelines more ubiquitous for different processes. See you in *Chapter 8!*

8

Powerful ETL Libraries and Tools in Python

Up to this point in the book, we have covered the fundamentals of building data pipelines. We've introduced some of Python's most common modules that can be utilized to establish rudimentary iterations of data pipelines. While this is a great place to start, these methods are far from the most realistic approach; there is no lack of space for improvement. There are several powerful, ETL-specific Python libraries and pipeline management platforms that we can use to our advantage to make more durable, scalable, and resilient data pipelines suitable for real-world deployment scenarios.

We will divide this chapter into two parts. We start by introducing six of Python's most popular ETL pipeline libraries. We will use the same "seed" ETL activities with each library, walking through how each of the following resources can be used to create an organized, reusable data ETL pipeline:

- Part 1 – ETL tools in Python:

  - Bonobo

  - Odo

  - mETL

  - Riko

  - pETL

  - Luigi

In the second part of this chapter, we will introduce a pipeline orchestration platform that can be used to establish robust data pipelines within a unified, scalable ecosystem:

- Part 2 – pipeline workflow management platforms in Python:

  - Apache Airflow

Technical requirements

To effectively utilize the resources and code examples provided in this chapter, ensure that your system meets the following technical requirements:

- Software requirements:

  - **Integrated Development Environment** (IDE): We recommend using PyCharm as the preferred IDE for working with Python, and we might make specific references to PyCharm throughout this chapter. However, you are free to use any Python-compatible IDE of your choice.

  - Jupyter Notebooks should be installed.

  - Python version 3.6 or higher should be installed.

  - Pipenv should be installed to manage dependencies.

- GitHub repository:

  The associated code and resources for this chapter can be found in the GitHub repository at `https://github.com/PacktPublishing/Building-ETL-Pipelines-with-Python`. Fork and clone the repository to your local machine.

Architecture of Python files

In the `chapter_08` directory in the GitHub repository, make sure the following files are within your directory:

```
├── Powerful_ETL_Tools_In_Python.ipynb
├── data
│   ├── traffic_crash_people.csv
│   ├── traffic_crash_vehicle.csv
│   └── traffic_crashes.csv
├── etl
│   ├── __init__.py
│   ├── extract.py
│   ├── transform.py
│   └── load.py
├── tools
│   ├── __init__.py
│   ├── 01_bonobo_pipeline.py
│   ├── 02_odo_pipeline.py
│   ├── 03_metl_pipeline.py
│   ├── 04_petl_pipeline.py
│   ├── 05_riko_pipeline.py
│   └── 06_luigi_pipeline.py
```

```
├── workflow
│   ├── __init__.py
│   └── airflow_pipeline.py
└── config.yaml
└── config.ini
```

The `extract.py`, `transform.py`, and `load.py` files are shown in the `chapter_08/etl` directory structure and perform the following functions:

- `extract.py`: Contains the `extract_data()` function that reads the CSV files and returns the DataFrames as a dictionary

- `transform.py`: Contains the `transform_data()` function that cleans, transforms, and merges the DataFrames, and returns the transformed data as a dictionary

- `load.py`: Contains the `load_data()` function that extracts and transforms the data, and loads it into the PostgreSQL database

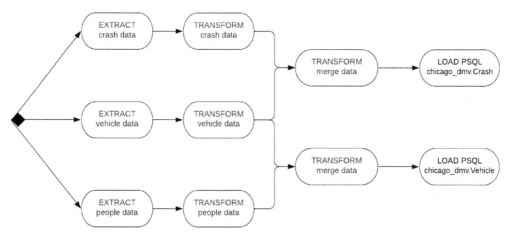

Figure 8.1: Diagram of demo ETL pipeline

In the preceding pipeline diagram, you can see that the pipeline starts by importing and transforming each of the data sources within the `/data` directory. Then, additional transformations are performed to merge data sources together to create the output data for the PSQL data tables, `chicago_dmv.Crash` and `chicago_dmv.Vehicle`. We will be using variations of the same ETL workflow to refactor each of the Python ETL modules to give you a clear *apples-to-apples* comparison of how each tool can be used to accomplish similar tasks.

To import the `extract.py`, `transform.py`, and `load.py` files in the `chapter_08/etl/` directory to your `p0#_<module>_pipeline.py` file, use the following syntax:

```
from chapter_08.etl.extract import extract_data
from chapter_08.etl.transform import (
    transform_crash_data,
    transform_vehicle_data,
    transform_people_data
)
from chapter_08.etl.load import load_data
```

Configuring your local environment

There are many ways to set up configuration files in your ETL project repositories. We will utilize two different forms, a `config.ini` file and a `config.yaml` file. Both work equally well, but we will use the `config.yaml` version more frequently. This is more of a "dealer's choice" situation than anything else.

config.ini

Open the `config.ini` file and replace `username` and `password` with the credentials for your local PostgreSQL environment:

```
[postgresql]
host = localhost
port = 5432
database = chicago_dmv
user = postgres
password = password
```

To import the `config.ini` file in the `chapter_08/` directory to your `p0#_<module>_pipeline.py` file, we will use the following syntax:

```
# Read the Configuration File
import configparser
config = configparser.ConfigParser()
config.read('config.ini')
```

config.yaml

Open the `config.yaml` file and perform the same task to replace `username` and `password` with the credentials for your local PostgreSQL environment:

```
# DISCLAIMER: modify the following code to match your local Postgre
instance
postgresql:
  host: localhost
  port: 5432
  username: postgres
  password: mypassword
  database_name: chicago_dmv
```

To import the `config.yaml` file in the `chapter_08/` directory to your `p0#_<module>_pipeline.py` file, use the following syntax:

```
# Import Configuration
import yaml
with open('../config.yaml', 'r') as file:
    config_data = yaml.safe_load(file)
```

Part 1 – ETL tools in Python

In your local environment, open the `Powerful_ETL_Tools_In_Python.ipynb` file using `jupyter notebook` in the command line in your PyCharm terminal.

Bonobo

Bonobo (`https://www.bonobo-project.org/`) is a Python-based **Extract, Transform, Load** (ETL) framework that uses a simple and rather elegant approach to pipeline construction. Bonobo treats any callable (i.e., function) or iterable object in Python as a node, which the module can then organize into graphs and structures to execute each object with simplicity. Bonobo makes it incredibly easy to build, test, and deploy pipelines, which allows you to focus on the business logic of your pipeline and not the underlying infrastructure.

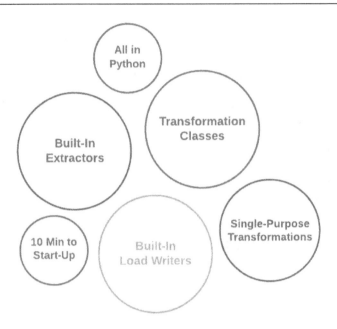

Figure 8.2: Bonobo is the Swiss Army knife for everyday data

Installing and using Bonobo in your environment

In your PyCharm terminal, install Bonobo using your `pipenv` environment with the following command:

```
pipenv install bonobo
```

Head to the `Powerful_ETL_Tools_In_Python.ipynb` notebook and take a look at the Bonobo section. You'll notice the following import:

```
import bonobo
```

To create a Bonobo pipeline, you must create a graph that will run each activity in a chain sequence:

```
def get_graph(**options):
    graph = bonobo.Graph()
    graph.add_chain(extract, transform, load)
    return graph
```

Then, create a parser object to get each aspect of the Bonobo graph in order to run the Bonobo ETL pipeline:

```
parser = bonobo.get_argument_parser()
with bonobo.parse_args(parser) as options:
    bonobo.run(get_graph(**options))
```

Creating a full ETL pipeline with Bonobo

To create an ETL pipeline with Bonobo, we first need to define the pipeline graph. Let's walk through how we came up with the following graph:

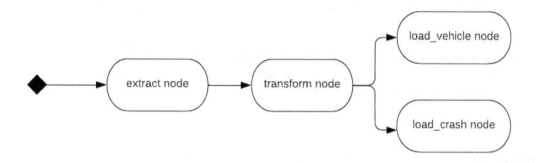

Figure 8.3: Bonobo pipeline diagram

Starting with the extract node (i.e., the contents of the extract.py file), which reads the data from the CSV files and returns a tuple of DataFrames, we modify the function to return a tuple value to pass to the transform node (i.e., the contents of the transform.py file) to then clean and transforms the data; finally, we pass the transformed data to the load_vehicle and load_crash nodes (split from the load.py file) to load the data into the corresponding tables in the PostgreSQL database.

Refactoring your ETL pipeline with Bonobo

In the chapter_08/tools/ directory, open the 01_bonobo_pipeline.py file in PyCharm.

The get_graph() function instantiates the Bonobo graph structure of the pipeline with Bonobo. graph() and then adds each node, the extract, transform, and load functions, to the pipeline using the graph.add_chain() method we saw earlier.

The if __name__ == '__main__' code block is also modified, which is now used to run the pipeline using the bonobo.run(**options) function. In this simple pipeline, we use relatively generic option parameters:

```
options = {
    'services': [],
    'plugins': [],
    'log_level': 'INFO',
    'log_handlers': [bonobo.logging.StreamHandler()],
    'use_colors': True,
    'graph': get_graph()
}
```

Feel free to play around with changing the options of the bonobo.run() function to see how it impacts your pipeline!

Overall, the refactored code in 01_bonobo_pipeline.py follows the same ETL workflow we saw at the beginning of the chapter. However, we add the Bonobo get_graph() function to create the nodes and graph pipeline architecture, and adjust the main() function to both create and run the new pipeline. We also add the add_chain() method to the extract, transform, and load activities (specified by the _input parameter) in order to append each task to the Bonobo graph. Finally, we run the Bonobo pipeline using the bonobo.run() function, with the ability to take in custom options specified in the options dictionary. Bonobo is an incredible resource when it comes to structuring your ETL data pipelines in Python.

Odo

Odo (http://odo.pydata.org/en/latest/index.html) is a Python library built on top of the Blaze and Dask libraries; it provides a uniform API for data migration between different formats, storage systems, and DataFrames. It accomplishes this by creating nodes of data formats that are connected via directed vectors indicating the transformation of one data type to another, and it supports migration between a wide range of formats, including CSV, JSON, Parquet, and SQL. The end result is a network of directed conversions, as shown in the complex diagram from Odo's documentation page. Most importantly, Odo handles data type conversion and data validation when converting between data types, making the data migration process easy and reliable.

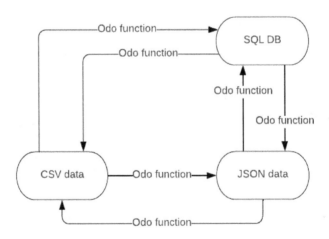

Figure 8.4: Odo: a web of connected functions

Installing and using Odo in your environment

In your PyCharm terminal, install `odo` using your `pipenv` environment with the following command:

```
pipenv install odo
```

Head to the `Powerful_ETL_Tools_In_Python.ipynb` notebook and take a look at the *Odo* section.

As we mentioned, earlier, each Odo function is represented by a single, directional, vector from one data type node to another. So, unlike Bonobo, we don't need to create a pipeline with Odo. Rather, the Odo function represents a single conversion of an object or string representation of the source data to the object or string representation of the sink data:

Figure 8.5: A single Odo function

Refactoring your ETL pipeline with Odo

In the `chapter_08/tools/` folder, open the `02_odo_pipeline.py` file in PyCharm. In this code file, we create odo functions to migrate data between the DataFrames and the PostgreSQL database. To do this, we add Odo "decorators" (`odo.odo()`) to each data step. For example, we can replace the `psycopg2` library with the `odo` library in the `load_data()` function:

```
postgre_config = 'postgresql://{user}:{password}@{host}:{port}/
{database}'.format(
    host=config.get('postgresql', 'host'),
    port=config.get('postgresql', 'port'),
    database=config.get('postgresql', 'database'),
    user=config.get('postgresql', 'user'),
    password=config.get('postgresql', 'password')
)
# Convert the dataframes to Postgresql tables using Odo
odo.odo(transformed_vehicle_df,
        config=postgre_config,
        dshape=config_data['vehicle_create_PSQL'],
        table=config_data['vehicle_table_PSQL'],
        if_exists='replace')
```

In the `02_odo_pipeline.py` file, you can see the constant use of the `odo.odo()` function. We successfully migrate the source data type, DataFrames, to the sink data type, PostgreSQL. Since the DataFrame is an object and the original data type, it's shown as the first argument of the function. However, since the output PostgreSQL is not an object in our environment, you'll see the PostgreSQL connection string as the second argument. We also added the `has_header` and `dshape` parameters to specify the format of the data being transformed between the two data types.

Overall, Odo is a powerful and flexible library that can simplify data migration in ETL pipelines, and make it easier to work with different data formats and storage systems. However, the immense flexibility of Odo is also one of its biggest drawbacks, as it can be a bit difficult to learn how to use it effectively. In the next section, we'll learn about a more lightweight module called mETL.

Mito ETL

Mito ETL (mETL) (`https://pypi.org/project/mETL/0.1.7.0dev/`) is a Python library that provides a simple, flexible, plug and play framework to manipulate *structured* source data to produce the specified *structured* sink data within the ETL workflow. It accomplishes this by providing a default list of 9 source types, 11 target types, and 35 of the most common transformation steps within the module. Though this is more restrictive than the previous two modules in this chapter, this module is significantly less complex and easier to use right away. Mito is designed to be lightweight and easy to use with a reduced learning curve compared to methods such as those discussed previously.

Installing and using mETL in your environment

One contingency of Mito is that it's a traditional Python package. While present within the `pipenv` environment (`https://pypi.org/project/mETL/`), it's not well maintained. In order to correctly install Mito in your internal environment, you will have to install this package directly into your local environment with `pip`:

```
pip install mETL
```

Head to the `Powerful_ETL_Tools_In_Python.ipynb` notebook and take a look at the Mito ETL section. In the code, you'll notice the following imports:

```
from metl.extractors.dataframe_extractor import DataframeExtractor
from metl.transformers.pandas_transformer import PandasTransformer
from metl.loaders.postgresql_loader import PostgreSQLLoader
```

The `DataframeExtractor()`, `PandasTransformer()`, and `PostgreSQLLoader()` mETL classes are used to construct the extract, transform, and load activity groups within an ETL pipeline. Each class in mETL coincides with the default list of source types, target types, and the most common ETL steps as mentioned earlier. These classes organize your code into beautifully formatted sections that are easy to use and maintain. As we said, this is a plug and play ETL module!

Refactoring your ETL pipeline with mETL

In the `chapter_08/tools/` directory, open the `03_metl_pipeline.py` file in PyCharm. In this code file, you'll notice how the entire pipeline is written into one `pipeline` variable using the `Pipeline()` class. The `Pipeline()` class takes each mETL pipeline as an ordered list, then runs the pipeline in sequence.

In this refactored code, we define the `load_data()` function as a mETL pipeline using the `Pipeline` class from the mETL library. We use Mito's `DataframeExtractor` class to load the CSV files into DataFrames, then perform various data cleaning and transformation operations on the DataFrames using Mito's `PandasTransformer` class. Lastly, we employ the `select_columns`, `merge_dataframes`, and `groupby` operations to transform the data into the required format for the PostgreSQL tables. Lastly, we use the `PostgreSQLLoader` class to load the DataFrames into the PostgreSQL database with the connection parameters and the table schema defined by the `dsn` and `tables` parameters, respectively, and the `primary_key` and `columns` parameters to define the table structure and constraints.

Overall, the mETL framework provides a powerful and flexible way to build ETL pipelines in Python, and can help to simplify and automate the data integration process in various data-driven applications. However, mETL's restrictions can become quite cumbersome if your data needs shift and change, and it lacks the functionality for streaming data integrations. In the next section, we will discuss how the powerful Riko module can tackle streaming ETL pipelines with ease.

Riko

Riko (`https://github.com/nerevu/riko`) is a Python library specifically catered to dealing with streaming data. As we mentioned earlier in the book, creating a pipeline to handle real-time streaming source data requires a specific process for cleaning and homogenizing the data into one cohesive data output. In most modern cases, a streaming data system requires cloud infrastructure and account for terabytes of data. However, if you're dealing with smaller amounts of data, comparable to the capacity of your local environment, using a module such as Riko can do the trick. Riko contains synchronous and asynchronous APIs, as well as supporting parallel processing, and states that it is well suited for processing **Rich Site Summary** (**RSS**) feeds related to the XML language used to create websites.

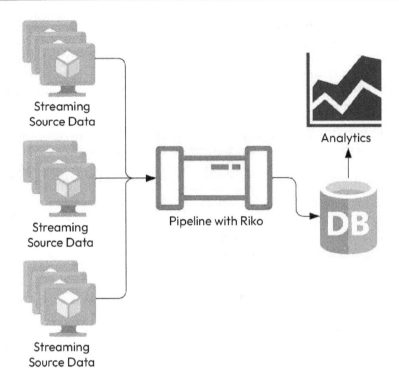

Figure 8.6: Example flow of pipelines with Riko

Installing and using Riko in your environment

Similar to mETL, Riko is present within the pip environment (https://pypi.org/project/riko/#installation) but, per the documentation, they do not recommend installing Riko into your virtual environment (https://virtualenv.pypa.io/en/latest/index.html), as some features are lacking. Thus, to install Riko into your local environment, enter the following command:

```
pip install riko
```

Head to the Powerful_ETL_Tools_In_Python.ipynb notebook and take a look at the Riko section. In the code, you'll notice the following imports:

```
from riko.modules import fetcg
from riko.sources import dict as riko_dict
from riko.sinks import sql as riko_sql
```

As you can see from the riko class structure, the core attributes are sources, sinks, and modules. Similar to the premise of mETL, the creator of riko (https://github.com/nerevu/riko)

built the module to handle 40 built-in modules, known as pipes, such as `csv`, `select`, `merge`, and `fetch`, to perform most pipeline tasks within the data streaming context.

For the specific pipeline we have been refactoring, we unfortunately will not need to utilize the true power of Riko. However, we highly encourage you to read through Riko's documentation to learn more about how to leverage streaming data.

Refactoring your ETL pipeline with Riko

In the `chapter_08/tools/`, open the `04_riko_pipeline.py` file in PyCharm.

In this refactored code, we utilize Riko's `dict` module to collect our sources into a single, iterable, dictionary. Then we use the `select`, `transform`, and `merge` modules to perform the data cleansing activities, clearly defining which transformation operations we want to perform on our dictionary of source datasets. This helps make our code more readable and consolidated, so it's easier for other engineers to peer review or debug, should the case arise. We finish off by utilizing Riko's `groupby` module to aggregate the data into the required format, and the `sql` module to load the data dictionaries into the PostgreSQL tables. With Riko, we were easily able to specify the database connection parameters and the table schema in the `dsn` and `columns` parameters, and we used the `primary_key` parameter to define the table constraints.

Overall, the Riko library offers an easy way to set up your pipeline to flexibly handle streaming data, enabling your pipeline to scale to a certain degree over the long term. Taking this approach during pipeline development can also help to simplify and automate the data integration process in various data-driven applications. In the next section, we introduce pETL, a Python module that focuses on ETL pipeline scalability.

pETL

pETL (`https://petl.readthedocs.io/en/stable/`) is a convenient Python library for building ETLs with various data source types (and data source quality). Using a marginal amount of your local system's memory, pETL focuses on scalability rather than processing speed. Thus, pETL is commonly used with smaller dataset sizes, so its greatest weakness is its lack of scalability to big data. pETL is particularly useful when you need to process and transform data from various sources before loading it into a target destination, such as a database or a data warehouse.

What makes pETL special is that it employs a lazy evaluation approach, meaning that operations are not executed immediately when they are called. Instead, they are stored as a sequence of operations that get executed when needed. This can help optimize memory usage and improve performance, especially for large datasets.

In addition to the built-in transformation functions, pETL allows you to define your own custom transformations using Python functions, giving you the flexibility to tailor the library to your specific needs.

Installing and using pETL in your environment

In your PyCharm terminal, install pETL using your `pipenv` environment with the following command:

```
pipenv install petl
```

Head to the `Powerful_ETL_Tools_In_Python.ipynb` notebook and take a look at the pETL section. You'll notice the following import:

```
import petl as etl
```

The transformation capabilities of pETL are at the core of its functionality. It offers a range of transformations to manipulate data including filtering rows, renaming columns, aggregating data, and joining data sources. In our example, you can see how easy it is to define simple transformation tasks such as `.convert('col_int', int)` and `.cutout('col_str')` in the readable and easy-to-follow syntax of pETL.

Refactoring your ETL pipeline with pETL

In the `chapter_08/tools/` directory, open the `05_petl_pipeline.py` file in PyCharm.

In this refactored code, we utilize pETL's `etl.fromdicts()` function to load the CSV files into dictionaries, in a similar fashion to how we used Riko in the previous chapter:

```
etl.todb(df_crash, config.get('postgresql', 'dsn'),
    'chicago_dmv.CRASH', create=True, schema=None,
    Commit=True, overwrite=False, error_handler=None,
    batch_size=None)
```

Additionally, we use the common `select`, `transform`, `join`, and `aggregate` ETL functions with the pETL module to perform data cleaning and transformation operations on the dictionaries. We then use the `todb()` function to load the dictionaries into the PostgreSQL tables, where we define the conditions for creating (`create`) or handling (`overwrite`) any present data to create or overwrite the database tables as needed:

```
etl.todb(df_crash, config.get('postgresql', 'dsn'),
    'chicago_dmv.CRASH', create=True, schema=None,
    Commit=True, overwrite=False, error_handler=None,
    batch_size=None)
```

Overall, pETL provides a powerful and intuitive way to build ETL pipelines in Python and can help to simplify and streamline the data integration process in various data-driven applications. Next, we will introduce a far more robust module, Luigi, that can be leveraged for complex batch jobs in ETL pipelines.

Luigi

Luigi (`https://luigi.readthedocs.io/en/stable/index.html`) is an open source Python package for building complex data pipelines of batch jobs. It was developed at Spotify to manage the organization's data workflows and has since become a popular tool for data engineering and data science teams.

With Luigi, you can define tasks as Python classes and specify their dependencies, inputs, outputs, and execution requirements. Luigi will then manage the task scheduling and execution, handling dependencies and ensuring that tasks are run in the correct order.

Some key features of Luigi include the following:

- **Task management**: Luigi provides a clear way to define tasks, their inputs, outputs, and dependencies, making it easy to understand the flow of your data pipeline

- **Dependency resolution**: Luigi automatically resolves dependencies and ensures that tasks are executed in the correct order

- **Workflow visualization**: Luigi has a built-in visualization tool that generates a visual representation of your workflow, making it easy to see the status of tasks and the progress of your pipeline

- **Flexibility**: Luigi provides a flexible framework for defining tasks and workflows, allowing you to customize your pipeline to your specific needs

To convert the existing ETL code to Luigi, we need to define Luigi tasks for each ETL step, specifying their inputs, outputs, and processing logic. We also need to define the task dependencies and the workflow structure, and run the Luigi scheduler to execute the tasks.

Installing and using Luigi in your environment

In your PyCharm terminal, install Luigi using your `pipenv` environment with the following command:

```
pipenv install luigi
```

Refactoring your ETL pipeline with Luigi

In the `chapter_08/tools/`, open the `06_luigi_pipeline.py` file in PyCharm. In this code, we define three tasks for each of the ETL steps: `ExtractCrashes`, `ExtractVehicles`, and `ExtractPeople` to read the data from the CSV files and filter the necessary columns; `TransformCrashes`, `TransformVehicles`, and `TransformPeople` to transform the data and output the cleaned CSV files; and `LoadCrashes`, `LoadVehicles`, and `LoadPeople` to load the data into PostgreSQL tables.

We also define a `ChicagoDMV` workflow task on line 132 that requires all the load tasks and runs the three load tasks, `LoadCrashes()`, `LoadVehicles()`, and `LoadPeople()`, in parallel:

```
class ChicagoDMV(luigi.Task):
    def requires(self):
        return [LoadCrashes(), LoadVehicles(), LoadPeople()]
```

To run the Luigi pipeline, you need to save the code as a Python script, for example, `06_luigi_pipeline.py`, and execute it from the command line using the `luigi` command. Before running the pipeline, make sure you have installed the necessary packages, such as `luigi`, `pandas`, and `psycopg2`, and configured the database connection in `config.yaml`:

```
luigi --module load ChicagoDMV --local-scheduler
```

This command will start the Luigi scheduler and run the `ChicagoDMV` Luigi task, specified by the `--module` option to run the load activities defined earlier in the script. The `--local-scheduler` option tells Luigi to use a local scheduler instead of a centralized one. If the pipeline runs successfully, you should see the data loaded into the PostgreSQL tables in the configured database, and the cleaned CSV files in the `data` directory.

Luigi is a good choice for small to medium-sized data pipelines with basic requirements and low complexity. However, when your pipeline construction and deployment exceed the realm of purely local development, this is where we need to transition to using ETL workflow management platforms.

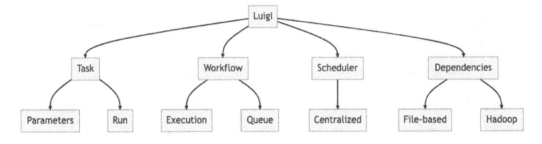

Figure 8.7: Example of a sample Luigi workflow

Part 2 – pipeline workflow management platforms in Python

All the Python modules we've introduced up to this point in the chapter are valuable tools to improve the efficacy and speed of Python data pipelines, but these modules won't solve everything. They do not provide a one-size-fits-all solution. As your data requirements expand, you will inevitably encounter the challenge of accommodating increasing capacity.

Pipeline workflow management platforms streamline and automate data pipeline deployments, and are particularly useful in scenarios where multiple tasks need to be executed in a specific order or in parallel, and where data needs to be transformed and passed between asynchronous stages of a given pipeline. There are a number of pipeline workflow management platforms available for Python. Here are some of the most popular ones:

- **Apache Airflow**: A platform to programmatically author, schedule, and monitor workflows

- **Apache Nifi**: An easy-to-use, powerful, and reliable system to process and distribute data

- **Prefect**: A platform for building, deploying, and managing workflows in Python

These platforms provide a range of features and functionality including task scheduling, dependency management, and data handling. They can help simplify the development and management of complex data pipelines, and are used by data engineers, data scientists, and developers in various industries.

In this book, we will limit our focus to Apache Airflow. However, we encourage you to read up on Apache Nifi (`https://nifi.apache.org/`) and Prefect (`https://www.prefect.io/`) on your own.

Airflow

Apache Airflow (`https://airflow.apache.org/`) is an open source platform that allows users to programmatically author, schedule, and monitor workflows. It was originally developed at Airbnb to help manage the company's complex data-processing pipelines.

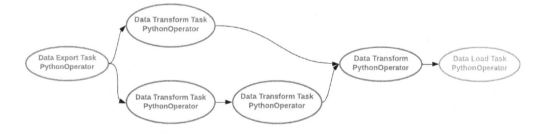

Figure 8.8: Example of an Apache Airflow Directed Acyclic Graph (DAG)

Airflow enables users to define workflows as code, allowing for version control, testing, and collaborative development. Workflows are built using a **Directed Acyclic Graph** (**DAG**) structure, which makes it easy to visualize the flow of data through the pipeline.

Airflow supports a wide range of data sources and destinations, including databases, cloud storage, and messaging systems. It also provides operators for common data processing tasks such as file manipulation, data transformation, and machine learning.

One of the key features of Airflow is its extensibility. Users can easily write custom operators or hooks to integrate with new systems or perform custom tasks. Airflow also has a rich ecosystem of plugins that provide additional functionality, such as integrations with cloud providers or third-party tools.

Airflow has a web interface that allows users to monitor the status of their workflows, view task logs, and manually trigger tasks if needed. It also supports email notifications and Slack integrations for alerting users to workflow failures.

Let's now see how we can convert an existing ETL code to Airflow.

Installing and developing with Airflow in your environment

One contingency of Airflow is that it's a traditional Python package. While present within the `pipenv` environment (`https://pypi.org/project/mETL/`), it's not well maintained. In order to correctly install Airflow in your internal environment, you will have to install this package directly into your local environment with `pip`:

```
pip install apache-airflow
```

Unlike the pure Python modules in the first portion of this book, to run the Airflow DAG, you need to connect to a web server or import your scripts directly into an Airflow workspace. For now, you can follow these steps to run your Airflow pipeline:

1. Start the Airflow web server by running the following command:

    ```
    airflow webserver
    ```

2. Start the Airflow scheduler by running the following command:

    ```
    airflow scheduler
    ```

3. Access the Airflow web interface at `http://localhost:8080` in your web browser.

4. Create a new DAG in the Airflow web interface by clicking on the **Create** button in the top menu and selecting **DAG**.

5. Define the DAG parameters:

    ```
    default_args = {
        'owner': 'first_airflow_pipeline',
        'depends_on_past': False,
        'retries': 3,
        'retry_delay': timedelta(minutes=5),
        'start_date': datetime(2023, 8, 13),
        'catchup': False,
        }
    ```

6. Define the tasks in the DAG by adding operators, such as `PythonOperator`, `BashOperator`, and `PostgresOperator`.

```
task_extract_crashes = PythonOperator(
    task_id='extract_crashes',
    python_callable =
        extract_data(config_data['crash_filepath']),
    dag=dag)
```

7. Define the task dependencies by using the `>>` operator to indicate which tasks should be executed after others:

```
task_extract_crashes >> task_transform_crashes
```

8. Save the DAG and start it by toggling the DAG switch to **On**.

9. Monitor the DAG status and the task logs in the Airflow web interface.

10. Test the DAG by running it manually or using triggers, such as sensors or external events.

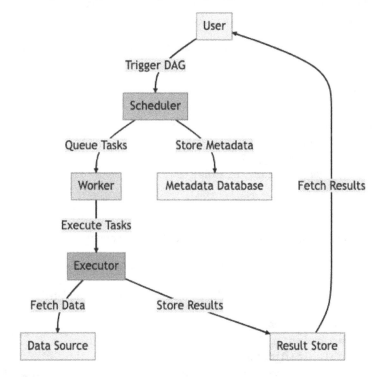

Figure 8.9: Apache Airflow in action

Refactoring your ETL pipeline with Airflow

In the `chapter_08/workflow/` directory, open the `airflow_pipeline.py` file in PyCharm. In this code, we start by defining the Airflow DAG parameters to define the `default_args` variable of the `chicago_dmv` Airflow DAG:

```
# Define the DAG
default_args = {
    'owner': 'first_airflow_pipeline',
    'depends_on_past': False,
    'start_date': datetime(2023, 8, 13),
    'retry_delay': timedelta(minutes=5),
    'catchup': False,
}
dag = DAG('chicago_dmv', default_args=default_args,
    schedule_interval=timedelta(days=1))
```

You'll notice that the `load_data()` function is the contents of the `chicago_dmv` Airflow DAG, which consists of several `PythonOperator` tasks.

We use the `PythonOperator` class to define the tasks, passing the function name and its arguments as parameters:

```
task_transform_crashes = PythonOperator(
    task_id='transform_crashes',
    python_callable=transform_crash_data,
    op_kwargs={'crash_df': "{{
        task_instance.xcom_pull(
            task_ids='extract_crashes') }}"},
    dag=dag
)
```

To feed the results of one task into another, we use the following syntax:

```
'df': "{{task_instance.xcom_pull(task_ids='transform_crash') }}"
```

This syntax is used in the `op_kwargs` list of the `PythonOperator` template:

```
task_load_crash = PythonOperator(
    task_id='load_crash',
    python_callable=load_data,
    op_kwargs={'df': "{{task_instance.xcom_pull(task_ids='transform_
crash') }}",
                'create_PSQL':
                    config_data['crash_create_PSQL'],
                'insert_PSQL':
```

```
                        config_data['crash_insert_PSQL']},
      dag=dag
  )
```

Once the `chicago_dmv` Airflow DAG contents are fully defined in `load_data()` function, we use the >> operator to define the task dependencies, indicating which task should be executed after another:

```
# Define the task dependencies
task_extract_crashes >> task_transform_crashes
task_extract_vehicles >> task_transform_vehicles
task_extract_people >> task_transform_people
task_transform_crashes >> task_load_crash
task_transform_vehicles >> task_load_vehicle
task_transform_people >> task_load_people
```

In summary, we use the `extract_` functions to read the CSV files and return Pandas DataFrames as the task results. We use the `transform_` functions to perform data cleaning and transformation operations on the DataFrames, using the XCom system to pass the results between tasks. We use the `load_` functions to load the DataFrames into the PostgreSQL database.

Overall, Airflow provides a powerful and flexible platform for building ETL pipelines in Python, allowing users to define, schedule, and monitor complex workflows with ease. It can help to streamline and automate the data integration process, making it more efficient, reliable, and scalable.

Summary

In this chapter, we went through a series of examples to demonstrate how to build robust ETL pipelines in Python using various frameworks and libraries.

By understanding the different frameworks and libraries available for building ETL pipelines in Python, data engineers and analysts can make informed decisions about how to optimize their workflows for efficiency, reliability, and maintainability. With the right tools and practices, ETL can be a powerful and streamlined process that enables organizations to leverage the full potential of their data assets.

In the next chapter, we will continue to dig deeper into creating robust data pipelines using external resources. More specifically, we will introduce the AWS ecosystem and demonstrate how you can leverage AWS to create exceptional, scalable, and cloud-based ETL pipelines.

Part 3:
Creating ETL Pipelines
in AWS

In the third part of this book, we will introduce Amazon's cloud computing service, AWS, and various strategies you can use to select the best tools and design patterns. We will learn how to create a development environment for AWS and how to use some automation techniques, such as CI/CD pipelines, to streamline production deployment.

This section contains the following chapters:

- *Chapter 9, A Primer on AWS Tools for ETL Processes*
- *Chapter 10, Tutorial – Creating ETL Pipelines in AWS*
- *Chapter 11, Building Robust Deployment Pipelines in AWS*

9

A Primer on AWS Tools for ETL Processes

We believe that with the right tools and practices, extract, transform, and load (ETL) can be a powerful and streamlined process that enables organizations to leverage the full potential of their data assets. As we've moved through this book, we've started to shift the emphasis from the thought process and general structure of developing simple data pipelines to researching and leveraging various Python modules or Python-specific interfaces to create more powerful data pipelines. Within this chapter, we again expand on this idea of working directly with cloud-based interfaces that are language agnostic.

Amazon Web Services (**AWS**) is one of the most widely used platforms for company data integration systems. Its flexible pay scale and wide range of applications and resources enable this platform to be equally useful for both large-scale corporations and small-scale side projects at home. Entire books have been written about AWS services, and most become quickly out of date due to the ubiquitous and quick-evolving nature of the AWS ecosystem. So, for the sake of this book, we want to focus solely on the Free Tier resources within AWS that you will use both at work and at home.

The chapter will proceed as follows:

- Common data storage tools in AWS

- Discussion—Building flexible applications in AWS

- Computing and automation with AWS

- AWS big data tools for ETL pipelines

- Walkthrough—Creating an AWS Free Tier account

- Command-line packages for a local AWS development environment

Common data storage tools in AWS

AWS provides a range of highly regarded data storage services, including Amazon **Relational Database Service** (**RDS**), Amazon Redshift, Amazon **Simple Storage Service** (**S3**), and Amazon **Elastic Compute Cloud** (**EC2**). These services are widely recognized and widely used in the industry for their reliability, scalability, and security.

Here is a list of tools that we are going to employ in this chapter:

AWS Tool	Use-Case Description
AWS Lambda	Run code without provisioning or managing servers. Great for event-driven data processing.
Amazon EC2	Provides scalable computing capacity in the cloud. Useful for running applications.
Amazon RDS	Managed relational database service. Suitable for structured data storage and retrieval.
Amazon S3	Object storage service. Ideal for storing and retrieving large amounts of data.
AWS Glue	Fully managed ETL service. Suitable for data cataloging and ETL jobs.
AWS Step Functions	Coordinate multiple AWS services into serverless workflows. Suitable for complex ETL tasks.
Amazon Kinesis	Collect, process, and analyze real-time data streams. Suitable for real-time analytics.
Amazon Redshift	Data warehouse service. Ideal for large-scale data analytics.
AWS Data Pipeline	Orchestrate and automate data movement and transformation. Suitable for complex ETL workflows.

Table 9.1: An overview of various AWS tools

Let's dive into each one of these tools.

Amazon RDS

Amazon RDS (`https://aws.amazon.com/free/database/`) is a fully managed relational database service that provides a flexible way to run and manage relational databases in the cloud. RDS supports various popular database engines such as MySQL, PostgreSQL, Oracle, SQL Server, and MariaDB. RDS provides features such as automatic backups, point-in-time restore, read replicas, multi-availability zone deployment, and integration with other AWS services such as S3, Glue, and Lambda. RDS provides a scalable and reliable platform for running various types of database workloads, such as **online transaction processing** (**OLTP**), **online analytical processing** (**OLAP**), or transaction processing.

Amazon Redshift

AWS Redshift (`https://aws.amazon.com/pm/redshift/`) is a fully managed data warehouse service that allows you to store and analyze large amounts of data in a scalable and cost-effective way. Redshift can be used as a target for ETL workflows that require aggregation, reporting, or data warehousing. It provides a SQL-based interface, automatic compression, distribution, backup, and integration with various **business intelligence** (**BI**) tools such as Tableau and Power BI.

Amazon S3

AWS S3 (`https://aws.amazon.com/pm/serv-s3/`) is a really awesome object storage service that provides an incredibly efficient way to store and retrieve data from anywhere in the world. So, given the right credentials, a user can store and retrieve any amount of data, at any time, from anywhere on the web, using a simple web service interface. Per its documentation, S3 is designed for 99.999999999% durability and 99.99% availability (that's a lot of 9s!) and provides unlimited storage capacity, with no minimum or maximum object size limits. S3 supports various data types and formats, including text, images, audio, video, and binary data, and provides features such as versioning, lifecycle policies, encryption, and access control. Due to this extreme level of flexibility and scalability, S3 is often used as a data lake or data hub, where data can be ingested, processed, and distributed to various applications and services.

Amazon EC2

AWS EC2 (`https://aws.amazon.com/pm/ec2/`) is a cloud service that provides virtual computing resources, such as CPU, memory, storage, and networking, on demand. EC2 allows users to quickly and easily launch and manage virtual servers (called instances) in the cloud, using a variety of operating systems, such as Linux, Windows, and macOS. EC2 provides a range of instance types, from general-purpose to high-performance, and offers various pricing options, including on-demand, reserved, and spot instances. Lastly, EC2 provides a scalable and reliable platform for running various types of applications, such as web servers, databases, and **machine learning** (**ML**) models.

By leveraging these AWS resources, organizations can easily manage their data storage needs, whether it be for relational databases with Amazon RDS, data warehousing with Amazon Redshift, object storage with Amazon S3, or scalable computing with Amazon EC2. AWS's comprehensive suite of data storage services empowers engineers to efficiently store, process, and analyze their data in a secure and scalable environment from any physical location.

Discussion – Building flexible applications in AWS

Before moving on to AWS applications used to help automate ETL development, we wanted to pause and discuss how to use AWS. S3 and EC2 instances are two core services offered by AWS that are frequently used together to build scalable and flexible applications in the cloud.

Leveraging S3 and EC2

Together, S3 and EC2 can be used in tandem to create a powerful and flexible platform for instantiating an application that is easily and reliably scalable in the cloud. S3 can be used as a storage backend for EC2 instances, where data can be stored and retrieved using S3 APIs, HTTP, or a CLI. By using S3 as the data source or target for ETL workflows, data can be ingested, processed, and stored in intermittent locations within different S3 buckets (such as staging and archive buckets). EC2 instances can then access the transformed output data from the S3 data directly over your network, without the need to copy or move data across credential walls. In the final use case for created data, such as dashboard visualizations for the business team, EC2 instances can be launched and managed using various tools and APIs, such as the AWS Management Console, the **AWS Command Line Interface** (**AWS CLI**), or SDKs, and can be integrated with other AWS services, such as **Elastic Load Balancing**, AWS Auto Scaling, or Amazon RDS.

Next are some examples of how S3 and EC2 instances can be utilized to create data pipelines.

Data ingestion

S3 can be used as a landing zone for data ingestion from various sources, such as **Internet of Things** (**IoT**) devices, logs, or batch processes. EC2 instances can be used to run custom scripts or applications that read data from the sources, transform it, and then upload it to S3. This data can then be stored and organized in S3 using different prefixes, folders, or bucket policies, depending on the data type and access requirements.

Data transformation

S3 can be used as a data store for intermediate or processed data that needs to be transformed, aggregated, or enriched. EC2 instances can be used to run ETL workflows that read data from S3, perform transformations using tools such as Apache Spark, Python, or SQL, and then write the results back to S3. This approach can be used for both batch and streaming processing, depending on data velocity and latency requirements.

Data analysis

S3 can be used as a data source or target for data analysis, using tools such as Amazon Athena, Amazon Redshift, or Apache Hive. EC2 instances can be used to run queries, generate reports, or visualize data using BI tools such as Tableau, Power BI, or Amazon QuickSight. This approach can be used for both ad hoc and scheduled analysis, depending on the business needs and data sources.

Data storage

S3 can be used as a long-term storage solution for data archiving, backup, or **disaster recovery** (**DR**). EC2 instances can be used to run backup scripts or tools that copy data from EC2 instances or other data sources to S3. This approach can provide a cost-effective and scalable solution for storing large volumes of data over a long period of time, with high durability and availability.

Overall, S3 and EC2 instances provide a flexible and scalable platform for building data pipelines that can handle various types of data and processing tasks. By leveraging the strengths of each service and integrating them with other AWS services such as Lambda, Glue, or EMR, data engineers and analysts can create end-to-end data pipelines that are efficient, reliable, and cost-effective.

Computing and automation with AWS

AWS Glue, AWS Lambda, and AWS Step Functions are three cloud services offered by AWS that provide serverless computing and workflow automation capabilities. Let's look at them in more detail.

AWS Glue

AWS Glue (`https://docs.aws.amazon.com/glue/latest/dg/what-is-glue.html`) is a fully consolidated data integration tool for end-to-end use, from data sourcing to analytic dashboards. It contains a fully managed ETL service that allows you to create and provide a number of features such as automatic schema discovery, data cataloging, job scheduling, error handling, and monitoring. Since Glue is an AWS service, it's integrated directly with over 70 types of source data formats as well as popular AWS data target locations, such as Amazon S3, Amazon RDS, and Amazon Redshift. Most importantly, Glue uses a serverless architecture that provides built-in **high availability** (**HA**) and pay-as-you-go billing for increased agility.

Within its infrastructure, Glue also supports various languages such as Python, Scala, and Java for creating custom transformations. It also contains a managed Apache Spark environment that can be used (at cost) to run PySpark or Scala workflows to process larger datasets using parallel processing within the cloud environment. Glue can be used to build scalable, reliable, and cost-effective data pipelines for various use cases, such as data warehousing, data migration, and data lake processing.

AWS Lambda

AWS Lambda (`https://aws.amazon.com/lambda/`) is a serverless compute service that allows you to run code in response to events or triggers, such as data changes in S3, DynamoDB, or Kinesis. Lambda can be used for simple ETL workflows that require real-time processing, filtering, or enrichment. It supports various languages such as Python, Node.js, and Java, and integrates with other AWS services such as S3, DynamoDB, and RDS.

This is a serverless computing service that enables developers to run code without provisioning or managing servers. Lambda supports various programming languages and can be triggered by various events such as API Gateway, S3, DynamoDB, or CloudWatch. Lambda provides a flexible and scalable platform for building event-driven and microservices architectures, where small pieces of code can be executed in response to specific events or requests and then scaled up or down automatically based on the workload. Lambda supports various features such as automatic scaling, monitoring, logging, and security, and can be integrated with other AWS services such as S3, EC2, or RDS.

AWS Step Functions

AWS Step Functions (`https://aws.amazon.com/step-functions/`) is a workflow automation service that enables developers to coordinate multiple Lambda functions, services, and tasks into a state machine. Step Functions provides a visual interface for defining and monitoring state machines, and supports various state types such as task, choice, wait, and parallel. Step Functions provides a scalable and reliable platform for building complex and long-running workflows, such as data processing, batch jobs, or business processes. Step Functions supports various features such as error handling, retries, timeouts, and input/output transformations, and can be integrated with other AWS services such as Lambda, **Simple Notification Service** (**SNS**), or DynamoDB.

Together or individually, Glue, Lambda, and Step Functions can be used to build serverless and event-driven workflows that automate various business processes and data workflows. *Glue* can be used to extract, transform, and load data from various sources into RDS databases, or to perform data processing and transformation using Spark and other tools. *Lambda* can be used to execute small pieces of code in response to specific events or requests and to perform data processing, transformations, or calculations. *Step Functions* can be used to coordinate and monitor multiple Lambda functions, services, and tasks and to manage complex and long-running workflows that involve multiple steps, branches, or conditions.

In addition to the foundational AWS resources, AWS also provides a robust suite of big data tools and services. These tools include Amazon EMR for processing large-scale datasets using popular frameworks such as Apache Spark and Hadoop, and Amazon Kinesis for real-time streaming data processing. With these powerful tools, businesses can effectively manage and analyze their big data workloads, gaining valuable insights and driving data-driven decision-making.

AWS big data tools for ETL pipelines

Several AWS tools can be used for creating ETL pipelines in the cloud. In this section, we chose to focus on the most common AWS tools that are best for building cost-effective and scalable ETL workflows.

AWS Data Pipeline

AWS Data Pipeline (`https://docs.aws.amazon.com/datapipeline/latest/DeveloperGuide/what-is-datapipeline.html`) is a web service for orchestrating data workflows across various AWS services and on-premises systems. It provides a visual pipeline designer that makes it easy to visualize and clearly define pre-built connectors for popular data sources and destinations, scheduling, error handling, and monitoring. Data Pipeline supports a wide range of data formats and protocols, including relational databases, NoSQL databases, and Hadoop clusters.

Amazon Kinesis

Amazon Kinesis (`https://aws.amazon.com/kinesis/`) is a managed service a big data platform specifically designed for processing large datasets (we're talking in the petabyte-scale range) for real-time data streaming and processing. Kinesis is one of Amazon's plug and play tools, so it's easy to start up and get your pipelines running. It provides a scalable and durable way to process and analyze data in real time, using Kinesis Data Streams, Kinesis Data Firehose, or Kinesis Data Analytics.

Amazon EMR

Amazon EMR (`https://aws.amazon.com/emr/`), formally known as Amazon Elastic MapReduce, is also a big data platform specifically designed for processing large datasets using Apache Hadoop, Apache Spark, and other open source tools. In comparison to Amazon Kinesis, which fills a similar role, EMR is far more flexible, but the onus is put on you to manage the infrastructure. EMR can be used for ETL workflows that require complex transformations, ML, or analytics, especially when dealing with large quantities of real-time data (think daily online sales for *Estée Lauder*). EMR is a scalable and cost-effective way to process this data in parallel using on-demand or spot instances.

These are some of the best AWS tools for creating ETL pipelines, depending on your specific needs and requirements. All three of the aforementioned services are easy to use, so the use of one over the other will be dependent on your specific needs, any cost limitations, and how each tool stands up in the face of your data source types and data sink requirements. With a bit more understanding about some of the tools within AWS you can use for larger data needs, we want to circle back to getting acquainted with AWS as a whole. In the next section, we walk through setting up your local environment for AWS; this starts off with signing up for a free account on AWS.

Walk-through – creating a Free Tier AWS account

When it comes to getting acquainted with a new cloud-based tool, the flexibility of a scalable environment can end up being your detriment since it is unfortunately quite easy to rack up unexpected charges while you play around with the new interface. In order to fuel that creative fire to learn while protecting your wallet from taking hits, we will keep things "free 99" during the exploration and learning period. Follow the next directions to create a Free Tier learning environment for yourself in AWS:

1. Head to `https://aws.amazon.com/free` and select the orange **Create a Free Account** button. Then, select the gray **Create a new AWS account** button.

2. Create a root user account with your email and AWS account name of your choice.

3. For the purpose of practice, make sure you create an account that is denoted as **Always Free** so that you can use all of AWS' tools within a specified processing power limitation to prevent the risk of unexpected charges.

If you would like to learn more about AWS Free Tier, please visit the following URL: `https://aws.amazon.com/free/free-tier-faqs/`.

In the following section, we'll go through connecting your new AWS account to your local environment for pipeline development. We'll go through case study use cases of AWS in later chapters; for now, we want you to familiarize yourself with working with AWS tools locally.

Command-line packages for a local AWS development environment

For developers working in a local environment, AWS provides command-line packages that enable seamless integration with AWS services. These packages, such as AWS CLI, allow developers to interact with AWS resources, manage infrastructure, deploy applications, and automate workflows directly from their CLI. With these tools, developers can leverage the full capabilities of AWS services without reliance on AWS's web **user interface** (**UI**).

Prerequisites for running AWS from your device in AWS

Using the **graphical UI** (**GUI**) of the AWS site is a great way to learn, but it makes for a clunky workflow when repeatedly establishing a development environment. To set up a local AWS development environment, we need to install several tools, including the following:

- **AWS CLI**—CLI for AWS services
- **AWS Serverless Application Model CLI** (**AWS SAM CLI**)—For building and deploying serverless applications
- **Docker**—Containerization platform for packaging and running applications
- **LocalStack**—Local AWS cloud environment for testing and developing applications

Each of the aforementioned tools plays an essential (or, at the very least, "strategically lazy") role in simulating your user access to the AWS online, GUI-restricted, interface on your own device. These tools also allow you to test your code before deploying it to the cloud, which will save you big bucks down the road. Next, we walk through how to install these tools to create an isolated AWS environment on your device.

AWS CLI

The purpose of the AWS CLI command-line shell program is exactly as the name suggests: it's a one-stop shop to control your entire AWS account from the command line. This means that there is no need for the GUI (at least, mostly).

To install AWS CLI, head to the following link: `https://aws.amazon.com/cli/`.

Verify the installation by running the following command in Command Prompt:

```
aws --version
```

Docker

Throughout this book, we've integrated the use of virtual environments into our development of ETL pipelines. The purpose of using virtual environments to contain modules was to prevent confounding factors, such as incompatible module-to-module circular dependencies, from interfering with how your data pipeline application deploys (in other words, preventing *dirty code*). The use of Docker containers and container images generally accomplishes the same thing: creating an isolated environment on your local system to deploy your applications.

The concept of a Docker "container" is very similar to the `pipenv` virtual environment we've been using in previous chapters, but with an added flair: it's deployable both locally and in the cloud. This means that you can set up a Docker container with all of the attributes for your data integration on one device, but using cloud deployment, it's also accessible from any device that contains access to that cloud environment. The runnable instance that gets deployed is called an *image*, which is the entirety of all configurations needed to run your pipelines. If a core configuration is only present on your local machine, such as credentials to an external database, Docker won't see it unless you add the same information to the deploying image because Docker only references the files and variables present within the image when deploying the container's data application on the cloud (or in an additional environment).

To install Docker on your local device, visit the Docker website and select the **Personal** (aka free) format of Docker: `https://www.docker.com/products/personal/`.

Open your iTerm2 terminal to verify your new installation of Docker is running with the following command:

```
docker --version
```

LocalStack

While not necessarily a requirement, LocalStack is a useful cloud service emulator that allows you to run everything related to single-container deployment (from AWS to Docker) from your command line. Feel free to play around with this feature in Docker, as desired.

To install LocalStack, run the following command in your iTerm2 terminal:

```
docker run --rm -it -p 4566:4566 -p 4571:4571 localstack/localstack
```

Verify the installation by running the following command in Command Prompt:

```
aws --endpoint-url=http://localhost:4566 s3 ls
```

AWS SAM CLI

AWS SAM is Amazon's open source framework for defining the infrastructure of your cloud environment. In layman's terms, this roughly translates to the foundational skeleton of your cloud computing environment. We won't go into the specifics of what options are available to you in this book, but feel free to read more about AWS SAM in its documentation: https://docs.aws.amazon.com/serverless-application-model/latest/developerguide/what-is-sam.html.

AWS SAM CLI is a command-line shell program that allows you to run the AWS SAM program locally. To install AWS SAM CLI, run the following command in your iTerm2 terminal (*Note*: we will use regular pip in this install instead of pipenv because we want it accessible on the entire device, not just in a single virtual environment):

```
pip install aws-sam-cli
```

Verify the installation by running the following command in Command Prompt:

```
sam --version
```

Summary

Within this chapter, we spent time reviewing some of the most popular resources within Amazon's cloud-based environment. With your local environment now configured to seamlessly integrate with AWS tools, you can harness the power of AWS cloud resources to enhance the scalability and resilience of your pipelines, even at their most basic level. This seamless integration opens up possibilities for adapting and optimizing your pipelines to leverage the robustness and scalability offered by AWS resources. We highly encourage you to spend a couple of hours continuing to explore some of the free offerings within AWS, as well as play around with solely relying on the CLI to get more comfortable with working with AWS from your local device.

Echoing our previous words of caution regarding the pros and cons of a scaling, pay-as-you-go price point, it can be just as dangerous as it is useful; keep in mind that you might shell out more money than you bargained for if you're not cognizant of what you're opting in for. We look forward to seeing you in *Chapter 10*, where we will start creating pipelines, starting from demo-sized to large-scale, in AWS.

10

Tutorial – Creating an ETL Pipeline in AWS

In today's cloud-based landscape, **Amazon Web Services** (**AWS**) offers a suite of tools that allows data engineers to build robust, scalable, and efficient ETL pipelines. In the previous chapter, we introduced you to some of AWS's most common resources within its platform, as well as set up your local environment for development with AWS tools. This chapter will guide you through the process of leveraging these tools, illustrating how to architect and implement an effective ETL pipeline in the AWS environment. We will walk you through the creation of a deployable ETL pipeline in Python Lambda Functions and AWS Step Functions. Finally, we'll create a scalable pipeline using Bonobo, EC2, and RDS. These tools will help all of your data pipelines harness the power of the cloud.

The chapter will cover the following topics:

- Creating a Python pipeline with AWS Lambda and Step Functions:

  - Setting up the AWS CLI in a local environment

  - Creating S3 buckets in AWS via the AWS console

  - Creating a Python script for each lambda function

  - Creating a JSON script for a state machine of Step Functions

- An introduction to a scalable ETL pipeline using Bonobo, EC2, and RDS:

  - S3 and EC2 instances – saving your Python code to your EC2 instance

Technical requirements

To effectively utilize the resources and code examples provided in this chapter, ensure that your system meets the following technical requirements:

- Software requirements:

  - **Integrated development environment** (**IDE**): We recommend using **PyCharm** as the preferred IDE for working with Python, and we might make specific references to PyCharm throughout this chapter. However, you are free to use any Python-compatible IDE of your choice.

  - Jupyter Notebooks should be installed.

  - Python version 3.6 or higher should be installed.

  - Pipenv should be installed for managing dependencies.

- GitHub repository: The associated code and resources for this chapter can be found in this book's GitHub repository at https://github.com/PacktPublishing/Building-ETL-Pipelines-with-Python. Fork and clone the repository to your local machine.

Creating a Python pipeline with Amazon S3, Lambda, and Step Functions

In this section, we will create a simple ETL pipeline using AWS Lambda and Step Functions. AWS Lambda is a serverless compute service that allows you to run code without provisioning or managing servers, while Step Functions provides a way to orchestrate the serverless lambda functions and other AWS services into workflows.

Setting the stage with the AWS CLI

Click into the chapter_10 directory of this book's GitHub repository in your local PyCharm environment. Within the PyCharm terminal, run the following command to configure the AWS CLI:

```
(Project) usr@project % aws configure
```

You will then be prompted to enter your access key ID, secret access key, default region name, and default output format. Use your internet browser to log in to your AWS management console to get the following credentials:

```
AWS Access Key ID [None]: <YOUR ACCESS KEY ID HERE>
AWS Secret Access Key [None]: <YOUR SECRET KEY ID HERE>
Default region name [None]: us-east-2
Default output format [None]: json
```

After you complete these steps, your AWS CLI is configured and ready to use. You can start running AWS CLI commands.

> **Note**
>
> Make sure you keep your AWS credentials confidential to protect your AWS resources. Avoid entering these credentials when using a public or shared computer.

Creating a "proof of concept" data pipeline in Python

Using AWS Services with Python is a combination of local development and cloud development. It's a good idea to have your pipeline's "proof of concept" written out and at least each chunk of code tested locally in a Python script prior to moving to AWS. This way, you have a pre-sanity check that your code performs as you expect it to before adding the complexity of working with a cloud environment.

For example, let's write a simple data pipeline that imports three CSVs, `traffic_crashes.csv`, `traffic_crash_vehicle.csv`, and `traffic_crash_people.csv`, as input data. The pipeline will import the files as individual DataFrames, then import each DataFrame by a specific list of columns (per DataFrame), and then return a dictionary that contains each DataFrame. In the following code block, you can see the "proof of concept" pipeline code that you can create in your local PyCharm environment. Maintaining all versions of the following code snippets in a GitHub-tracked repository is also recommended:

```
import pandas as pd

# Step 1: Read in Data
    crashes_df = pd.read_csv(path/to/my/ traffic_crashes.csv)
            ## repeat for vehicles_df and people_df

# Step 2: Filter dataframes by column lists
    filtered_crashes_df = crashes_df[['CRASH_UNIT_ID', 'CRASH_ID',
'CRASH_DATE']]
    filtered_vehicles_df = vehicles_df[['VEHICLE_ID', 'VEHICLE_MAKE',
'VEHICLE_MODEL', 'VEHICLE_YEAR', 'VEHICLE_TYPE']]
    filtered_people_df = people_df[['PERSON_ID', 'CRASH_ID', 'CRASH_
DATE', 'PERSON_TYPE', 'VEHICLE_ID', 'PERSON_SEX', 'PERSON_AGE']]

# Step 3: Place transformed data in dictionary for output
    transformed_content = {
        'crashes_df': filtered_crashes_df.to_csv(index=False),
        ## repeat for vehicles_df and people_df
```

Great! We've successfully defined the three main steps that our pipeline needs to perform. Now, let's make it conducive for the AWS environment. The first step is to upload our files to S3 storage.

Using Boto3 and Amazon S3 to read data

We introduced Amazon S3 previously in *Chapter 9*, but here's a quick refresher.

Amazon S3 is Amazon's web-based cloud storage service, designed for online backup and archiving of data and applications to make web-scale computing easier for developers:

In the following steps, we provide a high-level overview of setting up your S3 bucket through the AWS GUI:

1. Log in to the AWS management console, navigate to the S3 service, and click the **Create bucket** button.

2. Enter a unique name for your bucket (we will reference my-bucket-name in this chapter). This name must be globally unique across all of your AWS resources (Lambda functions, Step Functions, etc.).

3. Choose the region in which you want to create the bucket. This should be the same region as the rest of your AWS resources to minimize latency and data transfer costs.

4. Choose any additional options for your bucket, such as versioning, logging, or encryption. These options will depend on your specific use case and requirements.

5. Click **Create bucket** to create your bucket.

With your S3 bucket set up, we can now import our three CSV files in order to make them accessible within the AWS environment. To accomplish this, we can create a new file, upload_to_s3.py, and transfer the files using the boto3 Python package:

```
import boto3

# Step 1: Establish the boto3 s3 Client
s3 = boto3.client('s3')
bucket_name = 'your-bucket-name'

# Step 2: Define file paths within your local environment
crashes_path = 'path/to/my/traffic_crashes.csv'
## repeat for vehicles_path and people_path
# Step 3: Define output file paths within "my-bucket-name" s3 bucket
in a 'traffic' directory
crashes_key = 'traffic/traffic_crashes.csv'
## repeat for vehicles_key and people_key

# upload the file
s3. upload_file(Filename=crashes_path, Bucket=bucket_name,
Key=crashes_key)
  ## repeat for vehicles and people
```

With the files now imported into our S3 bucket, we can refactor our "proof of concept" data pipeline to reference the file paths in S3, instead of the local location:

```
import boto3
import pandas as pd

# Step 1: Establish the boto3 s3 Client
s3 = boto3.client('s3')
bucket_name = 'my-bucket-name'
# Step 2: Define file path within "my-bucket-name" s3 bucket
crashes_key = 'traffic/traffic_crashes.csv'
## repeat for vehicles_key and people_key

# Step 3: Use s3.get_object() to reference the file "object" in the s3
bucket
crashes_response = s3.get_object(Bucket=bucket_name, Key=crashes_key)
## repeat for vehicles_response and people_response

#  Step 4: Read in Data
crashes_df = pd.read_csv(crashes_response['Body'])
## repeat for vehicles_df and people_df
```

As you can see in the preceding code, we made some syntax changes to correctly reference each file's S3 bucket location on your server. This modification adds some additional steps to our original "proof of concept" pipeline, but this is how we migrate our pipeline to be functional within the AWS environment. With these changes, we can move on to creating AWS Lambda functions for our pipeline.

AWS Lambda functions

In this section, we'll explore how to use AWS Lambda functions to create modular steps within your ETL pipeline. By breaking down your pipeline into smaller, manageable steps, you can easily manage and optimize each step separately. This modular approach not only allows for easier debugging and maintenance but also offers flexibility in triggering different pipeline activities at different times. Particularly in cases where your code can be parallelized, this approach can significantly improve the efficiency of your pipeline.

AWS Lambda functions are essentially pods of Python code that represent one specific step within your pipeline. In other words, each lambda function corresponds to one step within your pipeline. This modular approach has several advantages:

- **Scalability**: By breaking up the processing cost of each step, it's easier for your pipeline to scale up and scale down resources between each step of your pipeline. This is especially useful for steps that require more computational power than others.

- **Flexibility**: This approach allows you, as the engineer, to trigger different pipeline activities at different times. This is particularly beneficial in circumstances where your code can be parallelized, as opposed to being run strictly in sequence.

Let's convert our code into Step Functions, based on the new pipeline format:

1. Establish the `boto3` S3 client:

```
import boto3
def lambda_handler(event, context):
    s3 = boto3.client('s3')
    return {"s3": s3, "bucket_name": 'my-bucket-name'}
```

2. Define the file path within the `my-bucket-name` S3 bucket:

```
def lambda_handler(event, context):
    bucket_name = event["bucket_name"]
    crashes_key = 'traffic/traffic_crashes.csv'
    ## repeat for vehicles_key and people_key

    return {"bucket_name": bucket_name,
            "crashes_key": crashes_key,
            "vehicles_key": vehicles_key,
            "people_key": people_key}
```

3. Use `s3.get_object()` to reference the file object in the S3 bucket:

```
def lambda_handler(event, context):
    s3 = boto3.client('s3')
    bucket_name = event["bucket_name"]
    crashes_key = event["crashes_key"]
     ## repeat for vehicles_key and people_key

    crashes_response = s3.get_object(Bucket=bucket_name,
Key=crashes_key)
     ## repeat for vehicles_response and people_response

    return {"crashes_response": crashes_response, "vehicles_
response": vehicles_response, "people_response": people_
response}
```

While it might be counter-intuitive, each of the preceding lambda functions must be defined within its own function file. Using the following directions, create a separate function file for each of the above lambda functions; we named these files `boto_function.py`, `s3_key_function.py`, and `s3_object_function.py`.

Adding lambda functions to AWS

Using the terminal in your PyCharm environment, convert each lambda function file to a ZIP file using the **command-line interface (CLI)** argument `zip`:

```
zip boto_function.py s3_key_function.py s3_object_function.py
```

Then, use the AWS CLI to create a new lambda function. You'll need to replace `<YOUR IAM ARN ROLE>` with the ARN of your IAM role found in your AWS console environment:

```
aws lambda create-function –boto-function UpperCaseFunction \
--zip-file fileb:// boto_function.zip --handler lambda_function.
lambda_handler \
--runtime python3.8 --role <YOUR IAM ARN ROLE>


aws lambda create-function –s3-key-function ReverseStringFunction \
--zip-file fileb:// s3_key_function.zip --handler lambda_function.
lambda_handler \
--runtime python3.8 --role <YOUR IAM ARN ROLE>


aws lambda create-function –s3-object-function ReverseStringFunction \
--zip-file fileb:// s3_object_function.zip --handler lambda_function.
lambda_handler \
--runtime python3.8 --role <YOUR IAM ARN ROLE>
```

Now that we have our Lambda functions available in our AWS environment, we can create a Step Function that will orchestrate the pipeline. The Step Function will define the flow of our pipeline and invoke the Lambda function at each step.

AWS Step Functions

In this section, we'll explore how to use AWS Step Functions to orchestrate and visualize your serverless ETL pipeline. Step Functions allows you to create a sequence of steps that define the flow of your pipeline, making it easier to organize and manage your pipeline as a whole. This approach allows you to clearly define the relationships between steps, making it easier to understand, modify, and maintain your pipeline over time.

Step Functions allows you to visualize and test your serverless applications. Similar to how each AWS Lambda function corresponds to one step of your data pipeline, each AWS Step Function corresponds to one lambda function. AWS Step Functions are defined in JSON format, which defines the sequence of steps (and the respective Lambda functions) in your pipeline. This approach has several advantages:

- **Visualization:** Step Functions provides a visual representation of your pipeline, making it easier to understand the flow of data and the relationships between different steps in your pipeline

- **Testing:** You can use Step Functions to test your pipeline and ensure that it works as expected before deploying it in a production environment

- **Maintenance**: Step Functions allows you to modify individual steps in your pipeline without affecting the entire pipeline, making it easier to maintain and update your pipeline over time

To create a Step Function, navigate to the Step Functions console in the AWS management console and click the **Create state machine** button. In the **State machine definition** section, define the flow of your pipeline using the JSON syntax with the **Amazon States Language (ASL)**, which is a JSON-based language. The following is an example of how you can convert your pipeline into the ASL:

```
{
  "Comment": "An example of a simple AWS Step Functions state machine
that orchestrates Lambda functions.",
  "StartAt": "EstablishS3Client",
  "States": {
    "EstablishS3Client": {
      "Type": "Task",
      "Resource": "arn:aws:lambda:REGION:ACCOUNT_ID:function:FUNCTION_
NAME",
      "Next": "DefineFilePaths"
    },
    "DefineFilePaths": {
      "Type": "Task",
      "Resource": "arn:aws:lambda:REGION:ACCOUNT_ID:function:FUNCTION_
NAME",
      "Next": "GetObjects"
    },
    "GetObjects": {
      "Type": "Task",
      "Resource": "arn:aws:lambda:REGION:ACCOUNT_ID:function:FUNCTION_
NAME",
      "End": true
    }
  }
}
```

In AWS, Step Functions are used to combine Lambda functions into one state machine for the pipeline. A state machine is triggered by Amazon CloudWatch, which is a fancy term for defining a pattern (or time-cadence) to run your data pipeline through AWS. To set up both a state machine and CloudWatch in AWS, follow these steps:

1. **Creating a State Machine via the AWS Step Functions Console**: Head to the AWS Step Functions console, and click **Create state machine**. Enter a name for your state machine (remember, you will have a different function for each lambda function, so name it accordingly) and choose

Standard as the type. In the **State machine definition** section, paste in the JSON code for your state machine and save it.

Alternatively, you can use the AWS CLI to create the state machine:

```
aws stepfunctions create-state-machine --definition file://
definition.json --name StringManipulationStateMachine --role-arn
<YOUR IAM ARN ROLE>
```

2. **Creating a CloudWatch trigger via the Amazon CloudWatch Console**: Navigate to the Amazon CloudWatch console and click **Create rule**. Choose **Event pattern** as the rule type. In the **Event pattern** section, choose **Build custom event pattern**. Define the criteria to trigger your ETL pipeline. For example, you can trigger the pipeline on a daily or weekly basis at a specific time. In the **Targets** section, choose **Lambda function** as the target type. Choose the AWS Lambda function that initiates your ETL pipeline and configure any additional settings (e.g., input data and role) as necessary.

Additionally, you can set up a cron job or other scheduling tool, locally, to run the pipeline at specific intervals or trigger it based on other events.

Once your pipeline has been converted to Lambda and Step Functions and uploaded to AWS in its totality, you can now run and deploy via the AWS CLI or within the AWS management console. Next, we will run through how we can scale our new AWS pipeline using additional AWS tools – namely, we will switch from using CSV files sourced from S3 within your local environment to using Amazon EC2 and Amazon RDS.

An introduction to a scalable ETL pipeline using Bonobo, EC2, and RDS

Extract, Transform, and Load (ETL) pipelines play a crucial role in data processing, enabling organizations to move data from multiple sources, process it, and load it into a data warehouse or other target system for analysis. However, as data volumes grow, so does the need for scalable ETL pipelines that can handle large amounts of data efficiently.

Amazon EC2 is a cloud service that provides virtual computing resources on-demand, offering a scalable and reliable platform to run various types of applications, including web servers, databases, and machine learning models. Amazon RDS is a fully managed relational database service that can be flexibly managed in the cloud, providing a scalable and reliable platform to run large database workloads.

When combined with an ETL-specific Python module such as Bonobo, Amazon EC2 and RDS can be leveraged to create an easily scalable data pipeline. This approach enables you to automatically increase or decrease computing capacity based on the needs of each pipeline deployment, ensuring optimal resource utilization and cost-effectiveness.

In the following section, we'll walk you through the steps to initiate a scalable ETL pipeline using Amazon EC2 and RDS with Bonobo.

Configuring your AWS environment with EC2 and RDS

To run a script using the EC2 and RDS tools, you need to first create instances of both through your AWS management console. Since we're dealing with databases, we'll stick to instructions via the GUI to maximize visualization.

Creating an RDS instance

Let's follow these steps:

1. From your AWS management console, navigate to the RDS service and click **Create database | PostgreSQL**.

2. Choose the following general-purpose configuration options:

    - **Instance Class**: `db.t3.medium`, with 8 vCPU and 64 GB of RAM

    - **Storage Type**: `SSD`, which is cost-effective storage that is suitable for a broad range of database workloads

3. Configure the security group, database name, master username, and password with the credentials required to connect and authenticate to your PostgreSQL database (refer back to the setup you created back in *Chapter 6*). This will allow your EC2 instance access to your PostgreSQL database. Click **Create database** to create your RDS instance.

Creating an EC2 instance

Let's check out the steps for creating an EC2 instance:

1. From your AWS management console, navigate to the EC2 service and click **Launch Instance**.

2. Choose the following general-purpose configuration options:

    - **Instance Class**: `t2.micro` – the free tier with 1 vCPU and 1 GB of RAM.

    - **Operating System (AMI)**: `Ubuntu SERVER 20.06 LTS AMI`.

    - **Storage Type**: `Amazon EBS` – essentially, a disk drive that can be attached to your EC2 instance.

    - **Network Settings**: `default VPC` – a **Virtual Private Cloud (VPC)** is an isolated cloud environment solely for your EC2 instance. By default, it is not reachable from the internet (that is, outside of your AWS environment).

- **Security**: Create a new security group to allow access to your RDS instance (and any other AWS tool you choose to add). By default, no inbound traffic is allowed until you add inbound rules to the security group.

3. Launch the instance.

Before moving on to the next section, make sure you download your key.pem file, which is the key to connect your EC2 to your local environment. Also, take note of your EC2 instance's IP address. You will use both of these to connect to your EC2 instance from your local environment.

Creating a data pipeline locally with Bonobo

To start, we need to convert our previous pipeline to use the Bonobo module to connect to your PostgreSQL database. In the GitHub repository, go into the chapter10/scalable-etl/ directory and open the my_pipeline.py file. At the top of the script, you will see the following import module section:

```
import pandas as pd
import psycopg2
import bonobo
from bonobo.config import use
from bonobo.constants import NOT_MODIFIED
```

At this point in the book, Bonobo won't be new to you (but here's a link to the docs if you need a quick refresher: http://docs.bonobo-project.org/en/master/index.html). However, we will use some different functions, use and NOT_MODIFIED, in this chapter. These features are known as *decorators*, and they help you annotate your code.

The NOT_MODIFIED decorator allows you to have the flexibility to use the created output data as the input data for any proceeding functions. This creates a "connection link" between functions so that the order of execution of them can easily be defined. You can see that we placed yield NOT_MODIFIED right after we defined the load() function to serve this purpose.

The use decorator helps flag dependencies in your workflow. So, before your script is able to make a Bonobo graph of your pipeline, each function of the pipeline must be run:

```
# Use Bonobo to define the pipeline workflow and dependencies:
@use("extract")
@use("transform")
@use("load")
```

To run the pipeline, you can use the following command in your EC2 instance. You can access the `my_pipeline.py` file from the GitHub repository. Please ensure that you update the file path to `chapter10/scalable-etl/my_pipeline.py` according to its location on your local machine:

```
(base) usr@project %   python -m bonobo run chapter10/scalable-etl/
my_pipeline.py
```

Adding the pipeline to AWS

As we mentioned previously, the EC2 environment is essentially its own, isolated, world out in the cloud. This means that it can't reference any dependencies that you've installed locally (i.e., Python and any associated modules). So, we need to create SSH into the EC2 instance to get the environment up to snuff.

Make your Python modules accessible within the EC2 instance. To SSH into your EC2 instance, use the `key.pem` file you downloaded when launching the EC2 instance, as well as the EC2 instance's IP address to connect from your command line:

```
(base) usr@project %   ssh -i /path/to/your/key.pem ubuntu@your-ec2-
instance-ip-address
```

Run an update on your EC2 instance with a `sudo` command for your EC2 Ubuntu server:

```
(base) usr@project %   sudo apt-get update
```

Install the necessary system packages and dependencies (e.g., Python, pip, Bonobo, and PostgreSQL):

```
(base) usr@project %   sudo install -y python3-pip
(base) usr@project %   pip3 install bonobos –user
(base) usr@project %   pip3 install psycopg2-binary --user
```

Transfer the data pipeline Python script to AWS using the `scp` command, which copies the script to the home directory (~) of your EC2 instance:

```
(base) usr@project %   scp -i /path/to/your/key.pem  chapter10/
scalable-etl/my_pipeline.py ubuntu@your-ec2-instance-ip-address:~
```

Now, you can run the files that are within your local environment through the EC2 instance, since the modules required for the script to run have been successfully imported into the EC2 cloud environment:

```
(base) usr@project %   cd ~(base) usr@project %    python3 my_pipeline.
py
```

Summary

In this chapter, we've taken a comprehensive journey of how to create both simple and scalable ETL pipelines with AWS, using both the AWS CLI for local development and the AWS management console to use the GUI interface. At first pass, the AWS environment can be a bit overwhelming, but with just a little practice, you'll start to feel a familiar flow between Amazon resources.

In *Chapter 11*, we will introduce the use of CI/CD pipelines, specifically tailored for ETL processes. We'll discuss the significance of CI/CD pipelines in automating code deployment and enhancing efficiency, reliability, and speed in your ETL process. You'll learn about AWS CodePipeline, AWS CodeDeploy, and AWS CodeCommit and how these services work together to create a robust and automated CI/CD pipeline for your ETL jobs.

11

Building Robust Deployment Pipelines in AWS

When creating a production-grade deployment environment, a robust **extract, transform, and load (ETL)** pipeline is just one vital component. To construct a solid foundation and structural framework for this environment, we need to implement CI/CD pipelines. **Continuous integration/continuous deployment (CI/CD)** pipelines for ETL enhance efficiency, reliability, and speed while ensuring a seamless and uninterrupted transition from development to production. In this chapter, we will go over how CI/CD tools enable engineers to automate code deployment with confidence, and we will establish an introductory CI/CD pipeline using AWS CodePipeline, AWS CodeDeploy, and AWS CodeCommit.

This chapter will proceed as follows:

- What is CI/CD and why is it important?
- Creating a robust CI/CD process for ETL pipelines in AWS
- Building an ETL pipeline using various AWS services

By the end of this chapter, you will know how to establish your own efficient CI/CD pipeline for ETL jobs using AWS CodePipeline, CodeDeploy, CodeCommit, and Terraform.

Technical requirements

To effectively utilize the resources and code examples provided in this chapter, ensure that your system meets the following technical requirements:

- Software requirements:

  - **Integrated development environment (IDE):**

  - We recommend using **PyCharm** as the preferred IDE for working with Python, and we might make specific references to PyCharm throughout this chapter. However, you are free to use any Python-compatible IDE of your choice.

  - Jupyter Notebooks should be installed.

  - Python version 3.6 or higher should be installed.

  - Pipenv should be installed for managing dependencies.

- GitHub repository: The associated code and resources for this chapter can be found in this book's GitHub repository at `https://github.com/PacktPublishing/Building-ETL-Pipelines-with-Python`. Fork and clone the repository to your local machine.

What is CI/CD and why is it important?

CI/CD automates testing to validate code changes and detect issues early in the development life cycle. Automated tests, such as unit tests, integration tests, and end-to-end tests, provide rapid feedback on the quality and functionality of your data pipelines. This skill set is usually handled by the development and operations teams (**DevOps**); however, if you're working as a data engineer on your own or part of a small company, you might have to wear the "DevOps hat" from time to time.

As a quick overview, CI/CD promotes faster development cycles, higher software quality, efficient collaboration, and a smoother deployment process, ultimately enabling organizations to deliver reliable software products more rapidly and with reduced risk. A CI/CD process can be visualized as a pipeline with each action the code deployment goes through forming an integral part of the whole. It establishes a resilient ETL process through four key aspects:

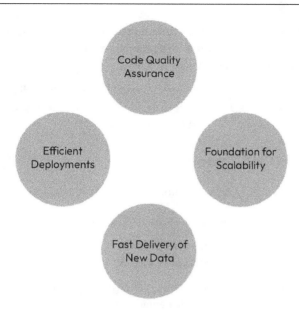

Figure 11.1: Diagram of the key ways CI/CD tests support the ETL process

In a nutshell, implementing CI/CD for ETL pipelines enables you to ensure data quality, streamline operations, and deliver data more quickly, making it a key element in creating a robust, effective ETL process. Let's dive into the concepts in detail.

The six key elements of CI/CD

Let's take a closer look at these six key elements:

- **Continuous integration (CI)**: CI involves consolidating all code updates into a centralized repository multiple times a day. This practice guarantees that everyone is working from the same code base, facilitating the early detection of conflicts.

- **Continuous deployment (CD)**: In CD, software is automatically launched into the production environment once it has successfully cleared all testing stages. This ensures that users always have access to the latest, bug-free version of the software.

- **Configuration management (CM)**: CM entails the oversight of all configurable elements of a software ecosystem, from versioning and hardware setups to environmental variables.

- **Infrastructure as Code (IaC)**: Using code to manage infrastructure elements such as servers and network configurations is known as IaC. This practice enables quick, reliable, and reproducible infrastructure setups and modifications.

- **Monitoring and notifications**: Actively monitoring the software system's performance and alerting the team about issues is crucial. This proactive approach allows for rapid identification and resolution of problems, minimizing user impact.

- **Collaborative culture**: CI/CD isn't just about methodologies and tools. It also involves fostering a collaborative culture between development and operations teams, commonly known as DevOps. This shared culture is pivotal for CI/CD success.

Essential steps for CI/CD adoption

If you're new to the world of CI/CD, here are some steps to help you begin:

- **Educate yourself**: Understand the various facets of CI/CD through online resources and literature.

- **Start incrementally**: Avoid the urge to adopt all elements at once. Begin with a couple of key aspects and expand your implementation as your comfort level grows.

- **Secure team commitment**: CI/CD requires collective effort. Ensure your team is supportive of the changes before you start the implementation process.

- **Select appropriate tools**: Numerous tools are available for facilitating CI/CD. Choose the ones that best suit your organization's specific needs.

- **Evaluate outcomes**: Continuously measure the efficacy of your CI/CD initiatives. This data will help you refine your processes and identify areas for improvement.

CI/CD is a continual process

Embarking on a CI/CD journey will steer your organization toward a more flexible and reliable development cycle. By focusing on the six pivotal elements mentioned previously, you're well on your way to enhancing the speed, quality, and dependability of your software releases.

CI/CD is a widely used toolset that finds applications across various roles in technology, including software engineers, data engineers, and DevOps engineers. While our discussion will primarily concentrate on its use in ETL pipelines, the principles we'll cover can easily be adapted for any coding project you may have:

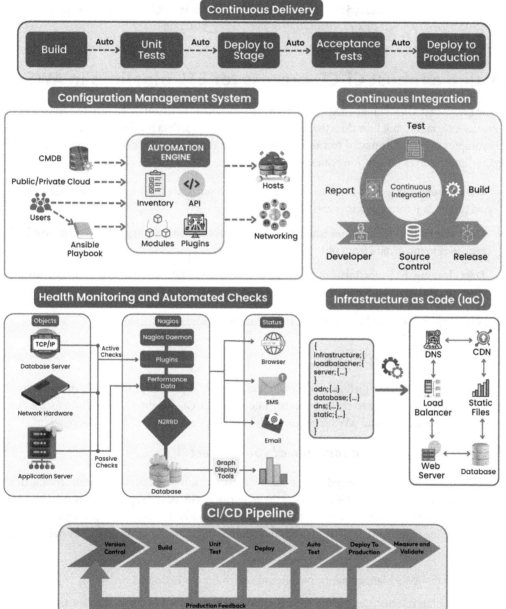

Figure 11.2: Diagram showing DevOps components

> **Attribution**
>
> *The six key elements of CI/CD* subsection and the *Figure 11.2* are excerpts from a LinkedIn post by one of the authors of this book, Brij Kishore Pandey (`https://www.linkedin.com/posts/brijpandeyji_6components-of-devops-that-can-help-you-activity-7095003211714953218-sgIe?utm_source`).

Creating a robust CI/CD process for ETL pipelines in AWS

We now know that CI/CD helps maintain high-quality software through automated testing and continuous integration. But how does that specifically apply to ETL data pipelines? Here, we'll provide brief examples of how automated testing reduces the chance of introducing bugs, facilitates early detection, and resolves integration issues in ETL data pipelines using AWS resources:

- **Data warehousing**: ETL processes are often used to pull data from several disparate sources and compile it into a single accessible warehouse

- **Data migration**: Companies undergoing digital transformation processes often use ETL pipelines to move data from old systems to new ones

- **Data cleaning**: ETL pipelines can be employed to clean, validate, and standardize data, ensuring it's in the right format for further analysis or processing

Let's put this into practice and create a CI/CD pipeline using tools within AWS.

Creating a CI/CD pipeline

The first step to building any pipeline is understanding the tools at your disposal. AWS provides a suite of services that work together to create a robust, automated CI/CD pipeline. This section focuses on introducing three fundamental AWS services: CodeCommit, CodeBuild, and CodeDeploy.

AWS CodeCommit – the foundation of your project

AWS CodeCommit is a fully managed source control service that hosts secure Git-based repositories. In short, it's Amazon's version of GitHub. Like the majority of Git-based repositories, CodeCommit allows multiple people to work on a project at the same time in a code base-controlled environment. To keep everything in the context of AWS, you can make an AWS CodeCommit service by performing the following steps:

1. Head to the AWS Management Console and search for `CodeCommit`.

2. In the region selector, choose the AWS Region where you want to create the repository.

3. From the dashboard, choose **Create repository**.

4. Under **Repository**, enter a name for the new repository (for example, `my-etl-repo`).

5. Click **Create**.

To seamlessly use Git commands in your local environment and interact with CodeCommit, adjust the `aws-codecommit-setup.sh` file in this chapter's code repository so that it matches your repository. Then, run the following commands in your PyCharm terminal:

```
chmod +x aws-codecommit-setup.sh
./setup_codecommit.sh
```

AWS CodeBuild – the workhorse of your pipeline

AWS CodeBuild is Amazon's fully managed CI/CD service that compiles your source code from AWS CodeCommit. CodeBuild is the environment where you can run CD tests over new code changes that are ready to be deployed. One caveat is that CodeBuild is designed to be used within the AWS cloud environment, so there's no straightforward way to run AWS CodeBuild in your local environment.

To connect a CodeBuild project to your CodeCommit repository, open the `buildspec.yml` file in this chapter's directory. This file defines the build steps and settings for AWS CodeBuild. We've provided a demo version of this file that can be customized to match the build requirements of your application.

You can make an AWS CodeBuild project by following these steps:

1. Head to the AWS Management Console and search for `CodeBuild`.
2. Click **Create build project**.
3. Name the project `my-etl-build` and provide an optional description.
4. Under **Source**, select **AWS CodeCommit** and choose the **my-etl-jobs** repository.
5. Under **Environment**, choose a suitable environment image.
6. Regarding Python scripts, choose **aws/codebuild/python:3.8.5**.
7. Under **Buildspec**, select **Use a buildspec file**. CodeBuild will automatically look for a file named `buildspec.yml` in your repository's root.
8. Click **Create build project**.

AWS CodeDeploy – the conductor of your orchestra

AWS CodeDeploy is a service that's designed to automate application deployments to Amazon EC2 instances, AWS Lambda functions, or on-premises servers. AWS CodeDeploy is tightly integrated with other AWS services and requires your application to be hosted on AWS infrastructure.

AWS CodeDeploy will handle the deployment process from CodeBuild to external environments for you. The setup involves creating and configuring deployment groups, application revisions, and deployment configurations, which are managed within the AWS cloud environment.

You can make an AWS CodeDeploy project by following these steps:

1. Head to the AWS Management Console and search for `CodeDeploy`.

2. Choose **Create application**. Name the application `my-etl-application`.

3. Select **EC2/On-premises** for **Compute platform**. Then, click **Create application** and then **Create deployment group**.

4. Under **Deployment settings**, choose **CodeDeployDefault.AllAtOnce**.

5. Click **Create deployment group**.

The following diagram depicts the workflow that we just discussed:

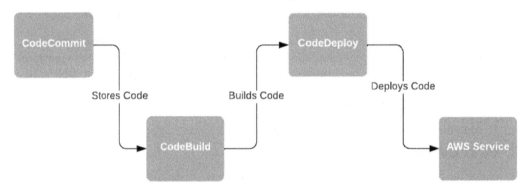

Figure 11.3: Diagram of the workflow of AWS CI/CD tools

As you can see, all of the CI/CD tools within AWS build on each other in a smooth, systematic fashion, making it flexible enough to accommodate any new needs that come up in your environment.

Building an ETL pipeline using various AWS services

With AWS CodeCommit, CodeBuild, and CodeDeploy set up in your environment, we can walk through how to build our CI/CD pipeline for ETL jobs.

Setting up a CodeCommit repository

As our first step, we'll initialize a new repository in AWS CodeCommit that will store the scripts for our ETL jobs.

Given your CodeCommit repository is named `my-etl-jobs`, clone the repository to your local system using the following command (replace `[region]` with your AWS Region):

```
git clone https://git-codecommit.[region].amazonaws.com/v1/repos/my-etl-jobs
```

Add demo-code in the etl directory to your CodeCommit repository:

```
git add etl/*
git commit -m "Initial commit of ETL script"
git push
```

Orchestrating with AWS CodePipeline

Now that we've created our repository, defined our build, and set up our deployment, we need a way to automate the whole process. This is where AWS CodePipeline comes in. AWS CodePipeline is a fully managed continuous delivery service that helps you automate your release pipelines for fast and reliable application and infrastructure updates. Let's create a pipeline that automates our CI/CD process:

1. Navigate to the AWS CodePipeline console and click **Create pipeline**.
2. Name the pipeline my-etl-pipeline and provide an optional description.
3. Under **Source**, select **AWS CodeCommit** and choose the my-etl-jobs repository.
4. Under **Build**, select AWS CodeBuild and choose the my-etl-build project.
5. Under **Deploy**, select **AWS CodeDeploy** and choose my-etl-application.
6. Click **Create pipeline**.

Your pipeline is now set up and ready to automate your ETL process, so every change pushed to your my-etl-jobs repository in CodeCommit will automatically trigger a build in CodeBuild. If the build is successful, CodeDeploy will deploy the built application.

Testing the pipeline

Let's test our pipeline by making a change to the etl.py script in our CodeCommit repository:

1. Make a change to etl.py on your local machine. It can be as simple as adding a comment.
2. Commit and push the change:

    ```sql
    git add .
    git commit -m "Test change"
    git push
    ```

As soon as you push the changes, navigate to the AWS CodePipeline console. You'll see that my-etl-pipeline has started a new execution. It will progress through the Source and Build stages and finally to the Deploy stage, where it will deploy your updated ETL job:

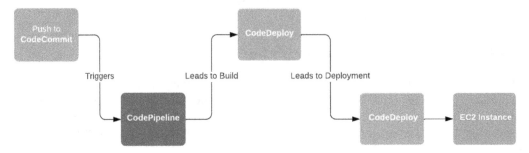

Figure 11.4: Diagram of how the AWS pipeline interacts with AWS CI/CD tools

This concludes the process of creating an automated CI/CD pipeline for your ETL jobs within the AWS ecosystem. You've now set up an infrastructure that will automatically build, test, and deploy your ETL code whenever a change is made, ensuring that your data pipeline remains up to date and robust.

Summary

Throughout this chapter, we have explored the capabilities of CI/CD tools in automating code deployment, how CI/CD tools can optimize our development workflows, and how they can be specifically tailored to various ETL processes. We also walked through a practical implementation of various AWS CI/CD services – CodePipeline, CodeDeploy, and CodeCommit – to create a foundation for your production-grade environment so that you can create more efficient, reliable, and scalable deployment workflows.

In the next chapter, we will transition from learning how to implement CI/CD pipelines to creating an effective orchestration of ETL pipeline deployment environments. Using CI/CD pipelines as the "silent structure," we will learn how to refactor a basic data pipeline so that it's both resilient and scalable by leveraging scaling and orchestration strategies.

Part 4:
Automating and
Scaling ETL Pipelines

In this last section of the book, we will start by covering how to create a robust ETL pipeline in AWS and apply scaling and orchestration strategies. We will introduce the fundamental testing strategies for ETL pipelines and how to both mitigate and quickly handle pipeline failures in a production environment. We will go on to discuss some of the industry's best practices for creating ETL pipelines in production, as well as identify some of the common pitfalls that engineers should avoid while building enterprise-grade data pipelines. Finally, we will close out this book with three practical case studies of how the tools we've introduced throughout this book can be applied to real-life data problems.

This section contains the following chapters:

12

Orchestration and Scaling in ETL Pipelines

When it comes to scalability, the orchestration of the data pipeline takes precedence. In the previous chapter, we introduced how CI/CD and design strategies can be leveraged to maintain data integrity and smooth pipeline deployments with external tools. In this chapter, we will explore how to orchestrate your ETL pipelines as the complexity and size of your data grows.

We'll explore important metrics for tracking your pipelines' health, such as latency, error rates, and data quality indicators, as well as various logging strategies that empower you to create a pipeline that is not only robust, but also easy to debug when errors inevitably arise in the future.

Specifically, this chapter will go through the following:

- The limits of traditional ETL pipelines
- Type of scaling
- Choosing a scaling strategy
- Data pipeline orchestration

Technical requirements

To effectively utilize the resources and code examples provided in this chapter, ensure that your system meets the following technical requirements:

- Software requirements:

  - **Integrated Development Environment** (**IDE**): We recommend using PyCharm as the preferred IDE for working with Python, and we might make specific references to PyCharm throughout this chapter. However, you are free to use any Python-compatible IDE of your choice.

  - Jupyter Notebooks should be installed.

  - Python version 3.6 or higher installed.

  - Pipenv is used for managing dependencies and should also be installed.

- GitHub repository:

  The associated code and resources for this chapter can be found in the GitHub repository at `https://github.com/PacktPublishing/Building-ETL-Pipelines-with-Python`. Fork and clone the repository to your local machine.

The limits of traditional ETL pipelines

Every system has its breaking point, and ETL pipelines are no exception. Traditional ETL pipelines were designed to handle data operations of a certain scale, and they do it well. However, the exponential growth of data and the need for near-real-time analytics have pushed these pipelines to their limits. Throughout this book, we have discussed the many limitations that non-scalable data pipelines face, so let's consolidate these limitations into four core groups here.

Performance bottlenecks

ETL processes are often heavy-duty operations. When data volumes soar, traditional pipelines can quickly become overwhelmed, leading to performance issues. These can result in increased latency, with data taking longer to be available for use, affecting downstream applications and decision-making processes.

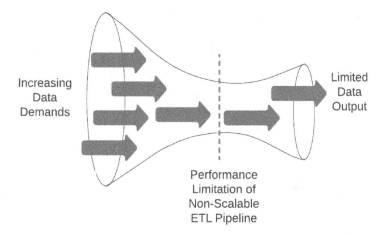

Figure 12.1: Visual example of performance bottleneck

Inflexibility

ETL pipelines, traditionally, have been hard to change. Modifications to accommodate new data sources, transformation logic, or loading strategies often require considerable effort, making them inflexible to evolving business needs.

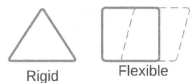

Figure 12.2: Visual example of rigid versus flexible construction

Limited scalability

While traditional ETL tools offer some degree of scalability, they generally struggle with large-scale data processing. The lack of horizontal scaling capabilities, in particular, can lead to stalled performance during peak data loads.

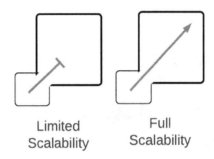

Figure 12.3: Visual example of limited versus full scalability

Operational overheads

Traditional ETL pipelines often require substantial manual effort for their operation, management, and troubleshooting. As data volume and complexity grow, these operational burdens can become unmanageable.

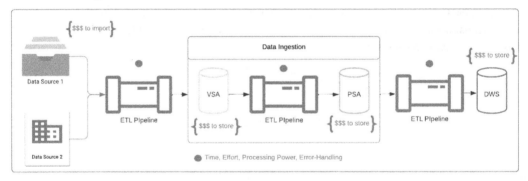

Figure 12.4: Visual example of operational overhead issues

Since we have discussed each of these categories of pipeline limitations throughout the book, you should be familiar with the premise behind the requirement for scalable ETL pipelines in the modern data world. We have also talked about various tools that you can use to create scalable pipelines in Python (think the Bonobo Python library and Amazon's cloud environment, AWS). In the next section, we will go over the two most common types of scaling categories: vertical and horizontal.

Exploring the types of scaling

When we talk about scaling in the context of ETL pipelines, it essentially means enhancing the pipeline to handle more data. There are two primary ways to achieve this – vertical scaling (scaling up) and horizontal scaling (scaling out).

Vertical scaling

Vertical scaling involves enhancing the capabilities of the existing system. It's called "scaling up" since it works by increasing the processing power of the current machine or node (i.e., in a Kubernetes cluster). This can range anything from simply updating the software of the machine to optimization configurations to even adding parallel processing within the same resource. Vertical scaling can be accomplished using physical hardware or cloud resources.

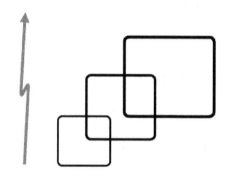

Figure 12.5: Visual representation of vertical scaling

The benefit of vertical scaling is that it's often straightforward to implement – you add more resources, and your pipeline runs faster. It ensures that you're using the maximum capacity of your current resources in the most efficient way (as is implied by optimizing the environment). In a perfect world, vertical scaling practices should be applied *before* moving on to adding additional resources, which could turn out to be an unnecessary additional expense. However, sometimes your data truly needs to scale beyond the physical limits of your current environment; that is when you transition to horizontal scaling.

Horizontal scaling

When you've reached the maximum processing capabilities of your environment, apply horizontal scaling by adding more machines (or cloud resources) to your pipeline's ecosystem. Also known as scaling out, horizontal scaling distributes the workload across multiple machines.

Figure 12.6: Visual representation of horizontal scaling

This type of scaling is particularly effective for processing large data volumes, as data and computations can be distributed across the nodes. However, while horizontal scaling allows virtually unlimited scalability, it usually comes not only with an economic cost; it also adds compounding levels of complexity to your pipeline. A highly parallelized system must manage data distribution, task synchronization, and error handling across multiple nodes, requiring specific tools and approaches. This is where pipeline logging, pipeline scheduling, and pipeline orchestration become increasingly important.

With a better understanding of the types of scaling under your belt, how do you decide which strategy is right for your data needs? In the next section, we will go over the logic of how to correctly choose your scaling strategy, and why it's appropriate to incorporate a balance of both types.

Choose your scaling strategy

The scaling strategy of your ETL pipeline environment is a critical decision informed by your specific use case, data characteristics, and operational constraints. While the list of factors to consider can be quite exhaustive, we have consolidated them into a list of the primary factors to consider when choosing a scaling strategy.

Processing requirements

If your ETL tasks are computationally intensive (e.g., complex transformations or machine learning models), vertical scaling can provide the necessary computational power. Processing requirement issues fall under the umbrella of bottleneck constraints; in order to resolve current issues and prevent future ones, you first need to start by monitoring and analyzing the resource utilization of your environment. For instance, if your pipeline is set up to run on a Kubernetes cluster, once you identify the nodes that are experiencing bottlenecks, you can simply increase the CPU capacity, memory, or disk space of those nodes by decreasing the capacity of other nodes that have extra to spare. However, it's important to monitor the performance and scale up cautiously to avoid over-provisioning.

Data volume

If your data volume is high and continues to grow, or is variable in any way, horizontal scaling can be a more sustainable approach. Handling variable data volumes is the "bread and butter" of cloud distributed systems. Kubernetes clusters with Apache Airflow or AWS **Elastic Container Service** (**ECS**) are designed to handle large data volumes by dividing the data and processing across multiple nodes.

Consider *FestiveCart*, a fictitious e-commerce platform. During last year's holiday sales, they had 1 million users visiting their site daily, generating approximately 2 TB of data per day. With their traditional on-premise solutions, the data-processing time increased from 2 hours to 12 hours, and they experienced two instances of system downtime. After migrating to a cloud-based ETL solution, they were able to manage the holiday data surge efficiently. The processing time remained constant at 2 hours, and no system downtime was reported.

Cost

Assessing the cost differences between vertical and horizontal scaling is highly variable and depends on depending on the specific ETL workload, data volumes, infrastructure setup, and cloud provider. Conducting a detailed cost analysis that takes into account your specific requirements and cost structure is essential for making an informed decision on the most cost-effective scaling approach for your ETL pipelines.

For instance, while vertical scaling can sometimes be simpler to implement, it can also be more costly. High-end machines with superior computational power can be expensive. Horizontal scaling, while introducing some complexity, can often be more cost-effective, particularly when using cloud-based systems where you can pay only for what you use.

HealthTrack Analytics, a fictitious healthcare analytics firm, saw a 40% spike in their cloud service bill over two months. Upon investigation, they found that redundant transformations—converting clinical data into different formats—were consuming a lot of resources. By optimizing these transformations and eliminating redundancies, the company was able to reduce its monthly cloud expenditure by 20%.

In summary, assessing the cost of scaling has no "one-size-fits-all" approach.

Complexity and skills

Horizontal scaling often requires a solid understanding of distributed systems, the adoption of which can increase the complexity of managing scaling. Converting your environment to run on Apache Hadoop and Spark pools, which sometimes requires converting your Python code to PySpark, can help manage this complexity. These environments also run on simple scripts; however, these environments also require their own specializations and therefore specific skills. If you're looking for a quick solution, factor in the time required for the learning curve.

Reliability and availability

Using distributed systems is a form of horizontal scalability, and they can often provide better reliability and availability. If one node fails, the system can often continue operating by redistributing the tasks to other nodes, as well as scaling up or down to match the data requirements of that particular run. This flexibility of processing resources adds both reliability and processing availability to the foundation of your pipeline ecosystem.

AgroSense, a fictitious start-up focusing on optimizing agricultural yields, started with 500 soil and weather sensors in a limited geographic area. Within a year, they scaled to 50,000 sensors spread over multiple states. Using cloud-based ETL, they were able to effortlessly scale their data processing from handling 50 GB of data per day to over 5 TB per day without any need for manual intervention.

Remember, choosing a scaling strategy is not a one-and-done decision. As your data and business needs evolve, you'll likely need to revisit and adjust your strategy. With our scaling options clear, we can now focus on the structural skeleton of your data pipeline: the pipeline orchestration.

Data pipeline orchestration

Having covered how to scale ETL pipelines, let's shift our focus to orchestrating them. If we think of our ETL pipeline as a production line, orchestration is about ensuring that each part of the line works in harmony, at the right time, and in the right order. Pipeline orchestration helps manage task synchronization as well as error handling in order to tie the entire pipeline process together into one clearly defined collection of resources.

Good orchestration can make your ETL pipelines more robust, efficient, and easier to manage. It involves several key elements:

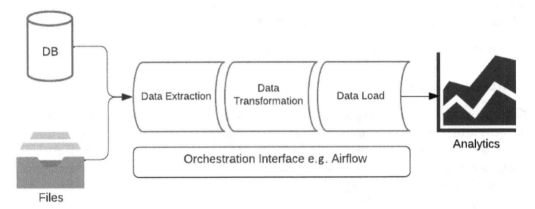

Figure 12.7: ETL pipeline with orchestration tool

Task scheduling

This refers to defining when and in what sequence ETL tasks are executed. For example, data extraction might need to occur before transformation and loading. Or, you might want to run some tasks during off-peak times to minimize system load. Tools such as Apache Airflow and Luigi are excellent for this purpose. They allow you to define complex workflows and schedules for your tasks, including dependencies between tasks.

Error handling and recovery

Even the best-designed ETL pipelines can encounter errors. Orchestration involves defining how to handle these errors. This could include automatic retries, skipping certain errors, or sending notifications for manual intervention. Good orchestration tools also provide capabilities for logging errors and tracking task progress, which can be invaluable for troubleshooting and recovery.

Resource management

With scaling, resource management becomes crucial. This involves ensuring that tasks have the necessary resources (CPU, memory, etc.) for their execution and that resources are used efficiently. For instance, you might want to limit the resources used by non-critical tasks during peak times to ensure that critical tasks have enough resources. Tools such as Kubernetes and Amazon ECS provide powerful features for managing resources in your ETL pipeline.

Monitoring and logging

Lastly, good orchestration includes monitoring your ETL pipelines and logging their activities. This can help identify bottlenecks, debug errors, and track the progress of ETL tasks. Most modern orchestration tools include features for monitoring and logging.

Putting it together with a practical example

Suppose you're working with a cloud-based ETL pipeline that uses Apache Spark for data processing. You chose to horizontally scale your ETL pipeline to handle growing data volumes from multiple sources. You use Apache Airflow for orchestration, defining a **Directed Acyclic Graph** (**DAG**) for your ETL tasks, scheduling them to run during off-peak hours, and setting up notifications for any task failures. You use Kubernetes for resource management, ensuring that your Spark jobs have the necessary resources while also maintaining efficiency. Throughout the pipeline, you monitor the task progress and log details for auditing and troubleshooting.

Such a setup represents a scalable, orchestrated ETL pipeline that can handle large data volumes efficiently, recover from failures, and is manageable even with the complexity introduced by scaling. This is the essence of modern ETL – a far cry from the rigid, limited ETL pipelines of yesteryear, and a necessary evolution in the age of big data.

In the following section, we present a sample code snippet to illustrate the fundamentals of a scalable ETL pipeline. This example can be easily customized to meet the specific needs of your project.

Understanding the concepts of data volume, cost, and scalability is critical, but nothing beats hands-on examples for learning. In this section, we'll bring it all together with a practical real-world example. We will build a simple ETL pipeline using Python and demonstrate how to orchestrate tasks.

Prerequisites

Before running the code, make sure you've installed the `psycopg2-binary` package using `pip`.

In this example, we'll walk through a simple ETL process that involves the following steps:

1. **Extract**: Read data from a CSV file into a Pandas DataFrame.
2. **Transform**: Filter rows based on certain conditions.
3. **Load**: Insert the transformed data into a PostgreSQL database.

This sample dataset is a simplified representation of a larger, more complex data source that you might encounter in real-life scenarios. We're using CSV for ease of demonstration.

Sample data

Let's consider a sample CSV file named `input_data.csv` with the following data:

```
id,name,value
1,Alice,5
2,Bob,11
3,Charlie,15
4,Diana,8
```

In the next section, we will create a sample ETL pipeline using Pandas and Postgres. The ETL pipeline will be built in Python, utilizing the Pandas library for data manipulation and the psycopg2 library for interacting with PostgreSQL.

Python ETL code

Create a new Python file called `etl_code.py` and include the following code to **transform** the data:

```python
import pandas as pd
import psycopg2
from psycopg2 import sql

# ETL task function
# Define a function called etl_task:
def etl_task():
    # Extract data from CSV
    df = pd.read_csv('input_data.csv')

    # Transform data : We filter rows where the value column exceeds
10.
    transformed_df = df[df['value'] > 10]
```

In the following code snippet, we'll establish a connection to a PostgreSQL database and proceed with data loading. Here, we establish a connection to the PostgreSQL database and insert the transformed data into a specified table. This is the **load** part of our ETL pipeline:

```python
# Load data into PostgreSQL
connection = psycopg2.connect(
        host="your_host",
        port="your_port",
        database="your_database",
        user="your_user",
        password="your_password"
)
cursor = connection.cursor()

for index, row in transformed_df.iterrows():
        insert_query = sql.SQL(
                "INSERT INTO your_table (id, name, value)
                VALUES (%s, %s, %s)"
        )
        cursor.execute(insert_query, (row['id'],
        row['name'], row['value']))

connection.commit()
cursor.close()
connection.close()
```

In the following section, we'll construct a sample DAG and set its schedule.

Apache Airflow DAG

Apache Airflow is used to orchestrate our ETL tasks. By defining a DAG, we can schedule and automate the pipeline.

Create a new Python file named etl_dag.py and place it in the dags folder of your Airflow installation:

```python
from datetime import datetime, timedelta
from airflow import DAG
from airflow.operators.python import PythonOperator
from etl_code import etl_task  # Importing our ETL task

# DAG definition
default_args = {
    'owner': 'airflow',
    'depends_on_past': False,
    'email_on_failure': False,
```

```
        'email_on_retry': False,
        'retries': 1,
        'retry_delay': timedelta(minutes=5),
}
```

We will create a DAG in the next code snippet:

```
# Here is how we can create a DAG and schedule an ETL task.
dag = DAG(
        'etl_dag',
        default_args=default_args,
        description='ETL pipeline using Python, Pandas,
        and PostgreSQL',
        schedule_interval=timedelta(hours=1),
        start_date=datetime(2023, 9, 5),
        catchup=False
)

etl_operator = PythonOperator(
        task_id='perform_etl',
        python_callable=etl_task,
        dag=dag
)
```

Note that to make sure to update the PostgreSQL connection parameters (your_host, your_port, your_database, your_user, your_password) and table name (your_table) in etl_code.py.

To execute this pipeline, place etl_dag.py in Airflow's dags folder and etl_code.py in a directory that's accessible to Airflow. Then, activate the DAG through the Airflow web interface.

This approach gives you a modular and cloud-agnostic ETL solution using Python and Apache Airflow for orchestration. You can directly insert this unified content into your book.

Summary

In this chapter, we explored the core concepts of orchestrating and scaling ETL pipelines, recognizing the need for efficient and scalable pipelines as data size and complexity continue to grow.

Effective orchestration ensures that ETL tasks are scheduled correctly, errors are appropriately handled, resources are efficiently managed, and progress is monitored and logged. By incorporating scalable and orchestrated approaches, organizations can overcome the limitations of traditional ETL pipelines, handle large data volumes, ensure efficient processing, and improve overall pipeline manageability and reliability in the era of big data.

As we close this chapter, we've set the stage for what comes next: rigorous ETL testing. In *Chapter 13*, we'll shift our focus to the different strategies and tools for ETL testing, aiming to further improve the performance and resilience of our pipelines.

13

Testing Strategies for ETL Pipelines

The main purpose of data pipelines is to facilitate the movement of information from its source to its destination. There is strength in this simplicity. But as we've seen throughout this book, pipelines have far more complexity under the hood, and this makes them equally prone to errors.

We've talked about how errors may arise from source data anomalies, transformation bugs, infrastructure hiccups, or a host of other reasons, but we haven't taken a deep dive into the structural components that data engineers can add to their pipeline ecosystem to ensure data integrity, reliability, and accuracy throughout the pipeline.

Testing data pipelines isn't a one-size-fits-all process, but it can certainly be a "one-size-fits-most" initial implementation. In this chapter, we will go through a few broad strategies that every data engineer should be familiar with, as well as the considerations to keep in mind while you're building your unit tests to create resilience throughout your pipeline environment. The chapter will cover the following topics:

- Benefits of testing data pipeline code
- Creating a testing ecosystem for data pipelines
- Best practices for a testing environment for ETL pipelines
- ETL testing challenges

Technical requirements

To effectively utilize the resources and code examples provided in this chapter, ensure that your system meets the following technical requirements:

- Software requirements:

  - **Integrated development environment (IDE):** We recommend using **PyCharm** as the preferred IDE for working with Python, and we might make specific references to PyCharm throughout this chapter. However, you are free to use any Python-compatible IDE of your choice.

  - Jupyter Notebooks should be installed.

  - Python version 3.6 or higher should be installed.

  - Pipenv should be installed for managing dependencies.

- GitHub repository:

  The associated code and resources for this chapter can be found in the GitHub repository here: `https://github.com/PacktPublishing/Building-ETL-Pipelines-with-Python`. Fork and clone the repository to your local machine.

Benefits of testing data pipeline code

Testing strategies for data pipelines are the unsung heroes behind successfully deployed data pipelines. They safeguard the quality, accuracy, and reliability of the data flowing through the pipelines. They act as a preventative shield, mitigating the risk of error propagation that could otherwise lead to downstream misuse of data. Thorough testing provides a sense of confidence in the system's resilience; knowing that the pipeline can efficiently recover from failures is a tremendous asset. Testing can also help efficiently identify bottlenecks and optimization opportunities, contributing to enhanced operational efficiency.

In this section, we will go over the most fundamental forms of testing strategies to implement in your data pipeline environments. The Python module `pytest` (`https://docs.pytest.org/en/7.3.x/`) is a popular functional testing package to use due to its readability as well as its ability to support both simple and complex functions.

> **Disclaimer**
> There are many different perspectives for creating a testing environment; some engineers prioritize pure tests and some prioritize cumulative tests. Most utilize both. Use the following examples to get familiar with creating tests for your pipeline, then proceed from there as you see fit.

How to choose the right testing strategies for your ETL pipeline

The following diagram displays the several areas of ETL testing employed for a robust data pipeline:

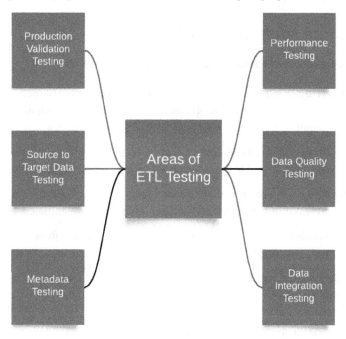

Figure 13.1: Areas of ETL testing

When choosing the right testing strategy for your ETL pipeline, there are a few factors to consider:

- **Project scope**: Small projects may be adequately served by unit tests and basic integration tests, while larger projects will need a more comprehensive approach, including end-to-end tests, validation tests, and performance tests

- **Data sensitivity**: If you are working with sensitive or regulated data, specialized tests aimed at ensuring compliance with laws such as GDPR or CCPA might be necessary

- **Team skillset**: The capabilities of your team can also guide your choice of testing strategy. Some strategies require specialized skills in performance testing, data validation, or security testing

- **Budget and time**: Comprehensive testing strategies provide better coverage but also require more time and resources

- **Nature of data**: If your pipeline handles a variety of data types, structures, and sizes, you'll need a diverse set of tests to ensure that all data is accurately processed

- **Existing tooling**: If your organization already uses certain tools for **continuous integration/ continuous deployment** (**CI/CD**), monitoring, or logging, consider how those can be integrated into your testing strategy

How often should you test your ETL pipeline?

Let's understand the frequency of tests needed in different testing methods:

- **Continuous testing**: For active projects, especially in **Agile** environments, you should be running your unit tests and smaller integration tests as frequently as possible — ideally, every time there's a commit
- **Scheduled testing**: End-to-end and performance tests are generally more time-consuming and expensive, so you might schedule them to run overnight or during other low-activity periods
- **Conditional testing**: Certain tests might be set to run only when specific conditions are met, such as after a certain number of new commits or when manually initiated
- **After data schema changes**: If the schema of your source or target databases changes, a complete run of all your tests is strongly advised
- **Regular monitoring**: Use tools such as **Prometheus**, **Grafana**, or **Datadog** to constantly monitor the pipeline and trigger certain tests if anomalies or errors are detected

Creating tests for a simple ETL pipeline

Let's create a simple pipeline with extract, transform, and load functions so we have something to work with. Take a moment to open the Jupyter Notebook associated with this chapter, `Testing_ Strategies_ETL_Pipelines.ipynb`. Take a look at the mini pipeline in the first cell:

Figure 13.2: Stages of ETL testing

Take note of the assumed data types, data structures, and premise of each function, then follow along with this chapter to make changes to the pipeline for each of the following testing strategies.

Unit testing

Unit testing is a type of testing designed to validate the functionality of individual functions in isolation from the rest of the data pipeline. It verifies that all individual functions and methods are working as expected. For example, "working as expected" usually relates directly to the data behaving in line with business expectations. If the purpose of a transformation activity in your pipeline is to simply double the input data, then assert that this is what occurs by creating a unit test. Here's how you might test this function using `pytest`:

```python
def test_transform_unittest():

    # define input and expected output data formats
    input_data = {'value': 5}
    expected_output = {'value': 10}

    # exercise
    result = transform(input_data)

    # verify
    assert result == expected_output,
    f'Expected {expected_output}, but got {result}'
```

Validation testing

To ensure that the data created from the pipeline matches expected results, create validation tests to check for data integrity and accuracy. In this test, we pass a negative value to the transform function and expect it to raise a `ValueError` with the `Value must be positive` message. We use the `pytest.raises` context manager to catch the exception and then check that it is as expected:

```python
def test_transform_validation():

    # define input data format
    input_data = {'value': -5}

    # define data condition for expectations
    with pytest.raises(ValueError) as excinfo:
        transform(input_data)
    assert str(excinfo.value) == 'Value must be positive.'
```

Integration testing

When seeking to test interconnections between the different components of the pipeline, we switch to using integration testing. ETL pipelines often involve complex transformations, including aggregations, joining multiple data sources, and intricate business rules. It can be challenging to reproduce these transformations accurately in a testing environment and to generate test data that covers all potential edge cases. Integration tests will help ensure that data can flow seamlessly from one end to the other without any disruptions. This test *asserts* that the transform and load functions are working together correctly to process and store the data:

```python
def test_load_transform_integration ():

    # define input and expected output data formats
    input_data = {'value': 5}
    expected_output = {'value': 10}

    # add transform and load
    transformed_data = transform(input_data)
    load(transformed_data, database)

    # verify
    assert database == expected_output, \
        f'Expected {expected_output}, but got {database}'
```

Disclaimer: In a more complex scenario, the transformation and loading steps might involve multiple functions, or even separate microservices. It's still important to test the integration points to ensure that data can flow smoothly from one step to the next.

End-to-end testing

End-to-end testing ensures the entire pipeline as a whole works as intended. It verifies that the pipeline correctly processes data from the input source to the final destination. In this test, we first create a setup with a test input file containing a random numerical string, 10, run the data through each step of the pipeline, and then *assert* that the output in the database is as expected:

```python
def test_pipeline_end_to_end():

    # define input and expected output data formats
    test_input_file = 'test_input.txt'
    expected_output = {'value': 20}

    # add open file to the test
    with open(test_input_file, 'w') as file:
        file.write('10')
```

```
# add extract, transform, load
input_data = extract(test_input_file)
transformed_data = transform(input_data)
load(transformed_data, database)

# verify
assert database == expected_output,
    f'Expected {expected_output}, but got {database}'
```

Performance testing

As pipelines scale, they become more complex and handle larger volumes of data. Performance testing gauges the scalability and speed of your pipeline, helping you catch any potential bottlenecks in your workflow. The following test uses the Python `test` module to gauge how long the `transform` function would take to process a large amount of data with your function. Getting a clear idea of the processing time will help you determine whether you can optimize your function or you need to add more resources to your pipeline:

```
import time

def test_transform_performance():

    # define input data formats
    input_data = [{'value': i} for i in range(1000000)]
# 1 million data points

    # define start time
    start_time = time.time()

    # integrate through the transform step
    for data in input_data:
        transform(data)

    # define the endtime
    end_time = time.time()
    elapsed_time = end_time - start_time
    print(f"Elapsed time for processing 1 million data
        points was {elapsed_time} seconds.")
```

For more detailed performance analysis or for tracking memory usage, you might want to use a more advanced profiling tool such as the `cProfile` module or a memory profiler package such as `memory_profiler`.

Resilience testing

Resilience testing is all about ensuring that your system can handle and recover from errors. This can involve a wide range of tests, from checking that your system handles incorrect inputs gracefully, to verifying that your system can resume operation after a simulated failure.

Let's consider a resilience test where we simulate a transient error in the transform step, such as a temporary network outage or a timeout error when accessing a remote resource:

```python
import random


def test_transform_resilience_timeout(input_data):
    """
    Transformation function to double the input value.
    Assumes input_data is a dictionary with 'value' key
    """

    # includes a random chance to raise a TimeoutError
    if random.random() < 0.1:  # 10% chance to raise an error
        raise TimeoutError('Temporary network outage.')

    output_data = {'value': input_data['value'] * 2}

    return output_data
```

We can write a resilience test that reruns the `transform()` function when it encounters a `TimeoutError` up to a maximum of five attempts:

```python
def test_transform_resilience_timeout_retry5():
    # Setup
    input_data = {'value': 5}
    expected_output = {'value': 10}

    # Exercise
    for i in range(5):
        try:
            result = transform(input_data)
            break
        except TimeoutError:
            if i == 4:  # We've reached our maximum attempts
                raise  # Re-raise the last exception
    else:
        raise ValueError("Transform function failed after 5
            attempts.")
```

```
# Verify
assert result == expected_output,
f'Expected {expected_output}, but got {result}'
```

In this test, we repeatedly call transform until it succeeds or we've made five attempts. If transform keeps failing, we eventually raise a `ValueError` to signal that the test has failed.

In a real-world scenario, your resilience tests might involve more complex error conditions and recovery strategies. However, the core idea is the same: simulate errors and ensure that your system can recover from them gracefully.

With a clearer understanding of the types of testing you use to improve the reliability of your pipeline environment, we now want to dive a bit deeper into the testing design structure.

Best practices for a testing environment for ETL pipelines

Like any ecosystem, each player in the group participates in altruistic, interactive relationships that build from the least complex to the most complex player. Since we need to establish a multi-layered testing strategy that covers everything from individual functions (unit testing) to the entire system (end-to-end testing), we need to discuss the key design principles for creating a testing ecosystem for data pipelines.

Defining testing objectives

Before writing any code, it's important to determine the *what* and *why* of your task. Why do you need testing in your pipeline? What do you want to achieve with your tests? Using the previous section as a reference, this can range from verifying data integrity or confirming data transformation accuracy to validating business rules or checking pipeline performance and resilience.

Establishing a testing framework

Choose a testing framework that aligns with your technology stack. For Python, you might choose `pytest`, which was discussed previously, or `unittest`, which we encourage you to investigate on your own (`https://docs.python.org/3/library/unittest.html`). Your framework should balance utilizing singularity tests (tests that serve a singular purpose) with offering utilities for setting up, tearing down, and isolating tests. To really solidify how all of these tests work together, we'll quickly review the premise of each test type and how they thread together in one altruistic ecosystem.

Unit tests

Think of unit tests as the smallest building blocks of testing the flow of data. A pure unit test validates *one* testable aspect of your pipeline, and *one aspect only*. As you saw in the previous section, these are the individual functions or classes that help you catch issues early in the development process and make debugging easier.

Integration tests

Integration tests are the next level up in complexity. How do the components that you just created for unit tests interact with each other? The premise of this type of test is to ensure that dataflows between components within the pipeline are functioning correctly. If something is awry between one function and another, an integration test should be there to detect it. So, for every function-to-function interaction, you will need to write an integration test.

End-to-end tests

End-to-end testing is the last layer of complexity that relates to data flow. Since these tests verify whether the entire pipeline works as expected, they help catch issues that might not be apparent when testing components in isolation. These are the "sanity check" tests that help you check the cohesiveness of your pipeline in short order.

Validation tests

Transitioning into other "sanity check" tests, validation tests make sure that the output of the pipeline is as expected, given some input. These tests ensure the accuracy and correctness of the data that your pipeline produces, which is how you build rapport and trust with the downstream users of your data.

Performance and resilience tests

How do you make sure your pipeline is scalable? Will your pipeline continue to perform as the processing unit requirements for your data pipeline expand? Will the pipeline be able to handle smaller than anticipated data amounts? Based on the anticipated needs and production conditions of your data pipeline, both performance and resilience tests cumulatively help to identify any bottlenecks or performance issues as well as ensure your pipeline can recover from errors or failures.

Automating ETL tests

Once your tests are in place, automate them. Running with the theme of strategic laziness, deploy your testing environment whenever any change is made to your pipeline (think pull requests for change branches into the `main` branch of your pipeline repository on GitHub). Automated tests can be run whenever changes are made to the pipeline, ensuring continuous testing. Powerful CI/CD tools automate the build, test, and deployment of your applications (see *Figure 13.3*):

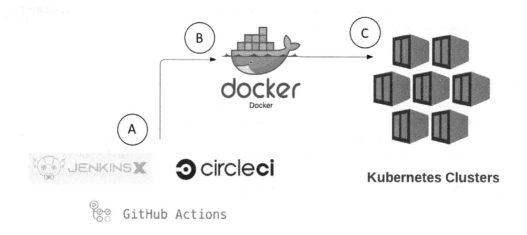

Figure 13.3: Example of how CI/CD tools can be applied and deployed

In the preceding diagram, you can see where CI/CD programs fall into the workflow of how to leverage CI/CD tools to automatically trigger a build process whenever changes are pushed or merged to the designated branch:

1. In a repository, before new code is added, the new code will first be scanned and approved by one of the pictured CI/CD tools, whose core responsibility is to test code changes based on the defined test within your environment.

2. To run a configuration file, engineers use a cloud tool such as **Docker** to outline the necessary steps to compile, package, and test the application. The CI tool will execute these steps and provide feedback on the build status, test results, and code quality.

3. Integrate your CI/CD tool with deployment automation tools such as **Kubernetes** to orchestrate the deployment process.

Depending on your company, especially in larger organizations, this might not be part of your job workflow. However, it's important to understand the general premise of CI/CD tools, so we'll provide a brief overview of the three most common CI/CD tools currently used in the industry: **Jenkins**, **CircleCI**, and **GitHub Actions**.

Jenkins

Jenkins (https://www.jenkins.io/) is an open source automation server that enables developers to build, test, and deploy their software. It is highly configurable and can be extended with hundreds of plugins, making it a flexible tool for CI/CD practices. You can configure Jenkins to automatically run tests every time code is pushed to your repository. If the tests pass, Jenkins could then build a Docker image with the new code, push that image to a Docker registry, and finally deploy it to a Kubernetes cluster. Any step of this pipeline can be fully customized, and Jenkins will notify you if anything goes wrong, allowing teams to find and fix problems quickly.

CircleCI

CircleCI (`https://circleci.com/`) is a popular CI/CD tool that relies on a YAML file within your repository that defines the pipeline configuration integration. CircleCI can be configured to install dependencies, run unit tests, and create a Docker image each time a new commit is pushed to the repository. If any step in this process fails, CircleCI will immediately halt further steps and notify the team, thereby reducing the time taken to detect and fix issues. It also supports parallel job execution, enabling quicker pipeline runs and faster feedback. Additionally, since it depends on a simple YAML file, CircleCI works seamlessly with GitHub and Bitbucket (`https://bitbucket.org/`).

GitHub Actions

GitHub Actions (`https://docs.github.com/en/actions`) is a CI/CD solution directly integrated into the GitHub platform. You can set up a GitHub Action to automatically run your test suite every time a new commit is pushed to your main branch. If a test fails, the Action can be configured to send an alert or even block the merge request until the issue is fixed. This integration of CI/CD directly into the GitHub platform allows for streamlined development workflows, reducing the overhead of managing separate tools and enabling quick and efficient delivery of robust software.

Monitoring ETL pipelines

Besides testing, also implement monitoring on your pipeline. Python has the capability to add monitoring to your data pipeline, similar to adding logging, as follows:

```python
def monitor_etl_pipeline():
    print("Monitoring ETL Pipeline...")
    try:
        # Extract data
        print("Extracting data...")
        extracted_data = extract_data()
        print("Data extracted successfully.")

        # Transform data
        print("Transforming data...")
        transformed_data = transform_data(extracted_data)
        print("Data transformed successfully.")

        # Load data
        print("Loading data...")
        load_data(transformed_data)
```

```
            # Pipeline executed successfully
            print("ETL Pipeline completed successfully.")

    except Exception as e:
        # Error occurred during pipeline execution
        print(f"ETL Pipeline failed. Error: {e}")
```

However, there are common online tools such as Prometheus, Grafana, and Datadog that have robust monitoring pipeline metrics. These can provide real-time feedback and alerts on the health of your pipeline. Additionally, regularly reviewing and updating your tests as your pipeline evolves will be an essential part of your development workflow. Keeping the test environment updated can be time-consuming, but it's essential for ensuring that your tests continue to provide value.

Remember, building a testing ecosystem for data pipelines is not a one-time task but an ongoing process. As your data, pipelines, and business needs evolve, so should your testing strategies. Maintain a culture of quality assurance and continuous improvement to ensure the reliability and effectiveness of your data pipelines. Notably, it becomes essential to address the unique challenges associated with ETL testing.

ETL testing challenges

Creating an ETL pipeline testing environment presents a unique set of challenges that extends beyond the quality and reliability of your data pipeline. We have discussed some of the potential errors to look out for, but there are additional confounding factors within your development and production environments that aren't as easy to debug by simply looking at your code.

Data privacy and security

Depending on the purpose of your ETL pipeline, you might be moving and transforming sensitive data. Creating a test environment that accurately represents this while complying with data privacy laws (such as GDPR or CCPA) can be challenging. Data masking or obfuscation techniques are techniques that are typically used to redact sensitive data in the lower environments (i.e., dev and test), but it can be challenging to accurately create versions of sensitive prod data that remains useful for development and optimization within these environments. It's important to write tests for data rules and requirements that match the production data, not just the dev/test data.

Environment parity

Maintaining a perfect mirror between the testing and production environments is crucial for accurate testing. This involves replicating not just the data, but also the hardware, software, network configurations, and even the system load. Any discrepancies between the test and production environments can lead to tests passing in one environment but failing in the other.

Overcoming these challenges involves careful planning, the use of automated testing tools, investing in scalable and secure test data management solutions, and continuously monitoring and updating your test environments.

Top ETL testing tools

The following are some of the most widely used ETL testing tools, each offering a unique set of features tailored to different testing needs:

- **Apache JMeter**: An open source performance testing tool for analyzing and measuring the performance of various services

  Best for: Load testing and functional testing

- **Talend**: Provides a wide range of data integration and transformation solutions, including data quality and testing

  Best for: End-to-end data integration and ETL testing

- **QuerySurge**: Focused on automating data testing, data validation, and data monitoring

  Best for: Enterprises looking for robust data validation and monitoring

- **QualiDI**: An end-to-end ETL test automation platform enabling enterprises to build a robust data testing framework

  Best for: Organizations seeking a unified platform for ETL development and testing

- **ICEDq**: Specializes in data testing for ETL and data migration projects

  Best for: Complex ETL processes that require stringent data quality and integrity checks

- **Tricentis Tosca**: An enterprise-level tool for functional and performance testing

  Best for: Organizations that require both UI and API testing capabilities

- **ETL Validator**: Designed to automate ETL testing, including data migration testing and data warehouse testing

  Best for: Automated regression testing and data migration validation

- **Informatica Data Validation**: Offers data validation and profiling features and can be integrated with **Informatica Data Quality**

  Best for: Large enterprises with complex data validation requirements

- **RightData**: Focuses on data quality assurance and data reconciliation

  Best for: Companies requiring continuous data quality monitoring

- **Assertible**: Designed for automated API tests, including web services and ETL processes

  Best for: ETL processes that involve complex API calls

These tools vary in features, cost, and complexity, allowing for a wide range of choices based on your project's specific needs.

Summary

Testing strategies for data pipelines are crucial for maintaining data integrity and pipeline efficiency in any data-centric organization. Given the diverse potential issues arising from source data, transformational bugs, or infrastructure problems, robust testing measures are indispensable. With the right approach, you can ensure the reliability and integrity of your data pipelines. It is likely that a combination of these different types of testing, tailored to the specific requirements and constraints of your pipeline, will significantly contribute to your organization's data-driven success.

Continuous monitoring is part of the testing strategy. In the next chapter, we'll explore important metrics for tracking your pipeline health, such as latency, error rates, and data quality indicators, as well as various logging strategies that empower you to create a pipeline that is not only robust but also easy to debug when errors inevitably arise in the future. To overcome these challenges, orchestration plays a crucial role in streamlining the ETL pipeline workflow.

14

Best Practices for ETL Pipelines

Up to this point in the book, we've gone through various tools and methods to create reliable, scalable, and maintainable ETL pipelines. We've also spent time discussing the concept of "*garbage in, garbage out,*" where the data quality and integrity of both the source and expected output data need to be prioritized throughout pipeline design and implementation, or the pipeline fails to perform its purpose. However, we haven't spent a significant amount of time discussing some of the most common pitfalls to be cognizant of while building these pipelines.

In this chapter, we will discuss the importance of monitoring and logging each activity process within every pipeline you build, and how error handling and recovery mechanisms will save you hours of frustration while debugging and troubleshooting a deployed pipeline. To create effective logging, we need to first discuss which aspects of your pipelines need to be tracked. The chapter will proceed as follows:

- Common pitfalls of ETL pipelines
- ETL logging in Python
- Checkpoint for recovery
- Avoiding **single points of failure** (SPOFs)
- Modularity and auditing

Technical requirements

To effectively utilize the resources and code examples provided in this chapter, ensure that your system meets the following technical requirements:

- Software requirements:

    - **Integrated development environment (IDE)**: We recommend using **PyCharm** as the preferred IDE for working with Python, and we might make specific references to PyCharm throughout this chapter. However, you are free to use any Python-compatible IDE of your choice.

    - Jupyter Notebooks should be installed.

    - Python version 3.6 or higher should be installed.

    - Pipenv should be installed for managing dependencies.

- GitHub repository:

    The associated code and resources for this chapter can be found in the GitHub repository: `https://github.com/PacktPublishing/Building-ETL-Pipelines-with-Python`. Fork and clone the repository to your local machine.

Common pitfalls of ETL pipelines

A "pitfall" refers to a disguised or concealed problem that can lead to your pipeline failing to accomplish its purpose. There is a profuse range of potential issues that can lead to pipeline failures, such as source data quality and compatibility (as we discussed back in *Chapter 5*), performance bottlenecks, and challenges with data privacy and security. The goal here is not to provide an exhaustive list, but rather to help train your mind to design your infrastructure to handle some of the most common pitfalls, as well as empower you to recognize potential "silent" (or concealed) errors that are unique to the specific technicalities of your data needs. In this way, you will be able to build ETL pipelines that are resilient, adaptable, and capable of driving data-driven decisions, while helping you navigate and avoid hurdles that could potentially derail your data engineering projects.

Data quality

In *Chapter 5*, we introduced the importance of maintaining data quality and designing your data pipeline to create the desired data output expectations; so, it should not come as a surprise that one of the most prevalent pitfalls is neglecting to consider data quality and validation checks at the point of extraction. If the ETL process does not correctly handle missing, inconsistent, or inaccurate data at the very start, the pipeline will contaminate downstream processes with poor-quality data. This can have an uncountable number of confounding issues due to making poor business decisions because of bad data and flawed information.

Since this oversight can lead to unexpected results when manipulating the data, returning incorrect results, or operations failing to perform due to type mismatch, let's take a look at how this plays out with an example about ignoring the data type during the extraction and transformation stages of an ETL process. In the following example, we import a `sales_data.csv` file, and the purpose of this transformation step is to calculate the sum of `sales` within that file:

```
import pandas as pd
df = pd.read_csv('data/sales_data.csv')
```

At first pass, it would seem reasonable to use the following code next:

```
total_sales = df['sales'].sum()
```

… but this relies on the data within the sales column being numeric values. Have we validated this? Nope. If the data is numerical, is it safe to assume that the data will always be numerical (and not in string format, for example)? Technically, also no. In practice, we should refrain from assuming that we can rely on data being in a specific format. So, in order to avoid the "pitfalls of data quality assumption," we need to add a data conversion step to guarantee that our data is in the correct format prior to transformation:

```
df['sales'] = pd.to_numeric(df['sales'], errors='coerce')
    # 'coerce' converts invalid values to NaN

total_sales = df['sales'].sum()
```

This is a great example of "defensive coding"—a strategy where you don't rely on assumptions and instead think about common pitfalls that might occur in your source data.

Poor scalability

In *Part 3*, we discussed various cloud services at your disposal for creating pipelines that scale to match the changes in data processing requirements per run. While this is great in practice, applying these tools correctly in reality is not always as straightforward. From our experience, the pitfall of poor scalability has less to do with not using a scalable environment and more to do with incorrectly planning for the future.

As you dig deeper into the world of data engineering, it is crucial to consider not just the volume of data pipelines can handle today but also what they might need to manage in the future. Data tends to grow exponentially in modern businesses, and ETL pipelines need to be prepared for this inevitability. The catastrophic system failure experienced by rigid pipelines is something we discussed at length in previous chapters. But we wanted to add an extra layer: creating a truly dynamic and scalable environment requires an engineer to think about both the needs of the present as well as the *anticipated* needs of the future (keyword: *anticipated*).

This is not an invitation to "plan for the worst" and scrape by on the pre-work of understanding the data problem your pipeline is seeking to resolve. It's an invitation to deeply understand the premise of your data problem and design your pipeline accordingly. For example, a data pipeline is to be deployed to record customer sales and initiate customer fulfillment pathways. This will require a vastly different range of scalability than a data pipeline that deploys to process company employee demographics and financial information on a monthly basis. The needs of these pipelines are inherently different, so using highly scalable (and more expensive) solutions for both would be a poor business decision.

Lack of error-handling and recovery methods

Lastly, and most relevant for this chapter, we wanted to highlight the *alarmingly common* pitfall of poor error-handling and recovery mechanisms. Real-word data is hardly as predictable and clean as perfectly curated development data. All of us are familiar with the feeling of designing a beautiful project within the safety of a development environment only to have our dreams thwarted by errors and failures when deploying our project in production. Even if prepared adequately, deployed pipelines can and will fail for a multitude of reasons. So, how do we create an environment where the root issue of a pipeline failure can be identified and resolved quickly?

This emphasizes the importance of creating a variety of logging activities to associate with each task within your data pipeline, as well as creating a systematic mechanism to alert the team about the failure as soon as it happens. Even with the best error-log alerts, there also needs to be a quick "recovery reset" for pipelines in production so that a previous implementation of the pipeline can be reinstated while the erroring pipeline is debugged. Let's dive a bit more into the "how" and "why" in the next two sections!

ETL logging in Python

Logging plays a crucial role in ETL pipelines, providing valuable insights into the execution and health of your data processing workflows. In this section, we will explore the importance of logging in Python-based ETL pipelines and discuss best practices for implementing robust logging mechanisms. As mentioned previously, as stewards of data, it is essential to have a clear understanding of what occurs during each stage of the ETL process. Logging provides a detailed record of events, including information about data sources, transformation steps, errors, and system performance, as illustrated in the following diagram:

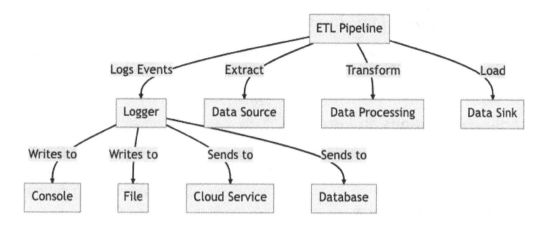

Figure 14.1: Processes that are logged in an ETL pipeline

In the following subsections, we will discuss some of the most important attributes of logging within your data pipelines.

Debugging and issue resolution

Logging enables you to identify and debug issues by providing insights into the state of both the pipeline and the data at various stages. Detailed logs help pinpoint the source of errors, track down data inconsistencies, and aid in the resolution of issues efficiently.

Auditing and compliance

Although we won't go deep into this topic in this book, it is important to remember that data is a source of currency, for both the company and individual data points in the dataset. Thus, in most industries, data compliance and auditing are essential. Logging helps maintain a clear record of data processing activities, ensuring that you can demonstrate data lineage, validate results, and meet regulatory requirements.

Performance monitoring

Monitoring pipeline performance is critical for maintaining efficiency and scalability. By logging key metrics such as data processing times, resource utilization, and data volumes, you can identify bottlenecks, optimize resource allocation, and improve overall pipeline performance.

Including contextual information

Enhance log messages by including contextual information such as input data details, transformation steps, and record counts. This contextual information aids in better understanding the pipeline's behavior and helps in troubleshooting.

Handling exceptions and errors

Properly handle exceptions and errors within your ETL pipeline and log relevant details. Include stack traces, error codes, and any other pertinent information that can assist in diagnosing and resolving issues.

The Goldilocks principle

The key to effective logging is to provide enough information to understand the what, when, and why of any event or error. Yet, at the same time, avoid logging excessively, as it may make it challenging to spot important details among a deluge of log messages. As with many things in programming and data engineering, the **Goldilocks principle** applies—your logging should be "just right."

Implementing logging in Python

In Python, the built-in `logging` module provides a flexible framework for emitting log messages from Python programs. In this section, we walk through a simple example of setting up a logger in an ETL process.

Run the following command to import the `logging` module:

```
import logging
```

To use the `logging` module, you start by creating a `logger` instance using the `.getLogger('name')` function, where `'name'` is a custom name for your `logger` instance that denotes the purpose of the logging instance:

```
logger = logging.getLogger('etl_logger')
```

Next, set the severity level of the `logger` instance. The Python `logging` module has five possible levels: DEBUG, INFO, WARNING, ERROR, and CRITICAL. The flexibility of this module allows engineers to build an environment of integrity that tracks changes in the progression of the pipeline without fixating on pipeline failures. For now, we simply want to see the logging information:

```
logger.setLevel(logging.INFO)
```

Next, create a `file_handler` instance with the `logging` module to define where the logging data is to be written. In the next example, we define the output location within the same directory of the pipeline by simply declaring the following filename: `etl_log.log`. Then, we define a `formatter` instance to define what is to be written in the `etl_log.log`. file, apply the `formatter` instance to the `file_handler` instance, and finally, add the `file_handler` instance of the `logger` instance:

```
file_handler = logging.FileHandler('etl_log.log')
formatter = logging.Formatter('%(asctime)s - %(name)s - %(levelname)
s - %(message)s')
file_handler.setFormatter(formatter)
logger.addHandler(file_handler)
```

Once the `logger` instance is fully calibrated, you can use `start` and `end` logging flags to wrap your ETL pipeline code in a similar fashion to what is shown here:

```
def etl_process():
    try:
            logger.info('Starting ETL process')
            # Your ETL code here...
            logger.info('ETL process completed
            successfully')
    except Exception as e:
            logger.error('ETL process failed',
            exc_info=True)
```

With a clear understanding of how logging can be applied to your data pipeline, it alludes to the issue of data flow. If one aspect of the data pipeline fails, such as a transformation activity, is the entire iteration of new data lost? Not for well-built pipelines. In the next section, we discuss how to create recovery checkpoints in your pipeline.

Checkpoint for recovery

A robust ETL pipeline is not just about moving data from point A to point B efficiently; it's also about ensuring that the pipeline can recover gracefully from failures and ensure data integrity throughout the process. To accomplish this, effective checkpointing needs to be incorporated with logging practices.

A "checkpoint" in the ETL process is a point in the data flow where key data cleansing and transformation processes "bookmark" the output data after each manipulation is stored in a temporary location. Thus, in the event of a failure, once the precise point of failure is identified, you can restart the ETL process from the last successful checkpoint, instead of from the beginning. This approach not only saves time and computational resources but also helps maintain data integrity by reducing the risk of duplicate or missed data. Using the same logging instance we defined earlier in this chapter, we can apply the same logging strategy to each function within the ETL pipeline instead of just around the full pipeline process, as follows:

```python
# Sample ETL functions
def extract():
    logger.info('Starting extraction')
      # extraction code here...
    logger.info('Extraction completed')

def transform():
    logger.info('Starting transformation')
      # transformation code here...
    logger.info('Transformation completed')

def load():
    logger.info('Starting load')
      # loading code here...
    logger.info('Load completed')

def etl_process():
    try:
            extract()
            transform()
            load()
            logger.info('ETL process completed successfully')
    except Exception as e:
            logger.error('ETL process failed',
            exc_info=True)
```

As we continue to improve our logging strategy, we want to take it one step further and discuss how to add a layer of protection to your pipeline by preventing points of failure.

The log file generated from the given code will contain timestamped entries indicating the start and completion of each stage (extract, transform, and load) in the ETL process. If the process runs without any exceptions, the log should indicate success at each stage. Otherwise, if an exception is encountered, it will log an error message along with the stack trace (because `exc_info=True` is set).

Here's a sample log file output:

```
2023-09-04 10:00:00,001 - INFO - Starting extraction
2023-09-04 10:00:05,123 - INFO - Extraction completed
2023-09-04 10:00:05,124 - INFO - Starting transformation
2023-09-04 10:00:10,789 - INFO - Transformation completed
2023-09-04 10:00:10,790 - INFO - Starting load
2023-09-04 10:00:15,456 - INFO - Load completed
2023-09-04 10:00:15,457 - INFO - ETL process completed successfully
```

If there's an exception—for example, during the transformation stage—the log would look like this:

```
2023-09-04 10:00:00,001 - INFO - Starting extraction
2023-09-04 10:00:05,123 - INFO - Extraction completed
2023-09-04 10:00:05,124 - INFO - Starting transformation
2023-09-04 10:00:06,567 - ERROR - ETL process failed
Traceback (most recent call last):
  File "<your_code_file>", line xx, in etl_process
    transform()
  File "<your_code_file>", line xx, in transform
    # some error here
Exception: <Description of the exception>
```

Note that the timestamps and line numbers are just for demonstration and will vary in your actual log file. The logger's format and the file's layout could also be different based on your logger configuration.

Avoiding SPOFs

A SPOF in a data pipeline is a part of the system that, if it fails, will stop the entire system from working. SPOFs can severely impact the reliability and availability of your pipeline, leading to data processing delays, loss of data, and disruptions in downstream analytics. Avoiding SPOFs involves implementing redundancy and fault tolerance in your data pipeline design. Redundancy means having backup resources to take over if the primary resource fails. Fault tolerance involves designing the system to continue operation, even in a degraded state, when some part of the system fails.

Using the same `logger` instance as before, let's add some redundancy to the `extract()` function of our demo data pipeline. To do this, we create two extract functions: `extract_from_source1()` and `extract_from_source2()`. Both functions import the same data source, but the second function is only run if the first function fails:

```
def extract():
    try:
        logger.info('Starting extraction from Source 1')
        extract_from_source1()
```

```
        logger.info('Extraction from Source 1
        completed')
    except Exception as e:
        logger.error('Failed to extract from Source 1',
        exc_info=True)
        try:
            logger.info('Starting extraction from
            Source 2')
            extract_from_source2()
            logger.info('Extraction from Source 2
            completed')
        except Exception as e:
            logger.error('Failed to extract from
            Source 2', exc_info=True)
            raise
```

In addition to preventing SPOFs, a robust pipeline will also keep track of consistent errors, warnings, or hiccups that typically occur during the progression of your pipeline runs.

Modularity and auditing

In the real world, most data (especially *interesting* data) is tracked and monitored to ensure it's shared and used correctly. This is crucial for traceability, debugging, and ensuring compliance with data governance policies, industry standards, or general cohesion between data output across departments. We've referenced the importance of creating a beautiful, **DRY** (which stands for **don't repeat yourself**) coding environment for your pipeline as well as a balanced, Goldilocks logging strategy, but **modularity** and **auditing** take these concepts to a new level. When used in tandem, modularity and auditing create efficient, maintainable, and transparent data pipelines.

Modularity

Modularity is the concept of breaking down your code into modular components in order to reduce the complexity of your code. There's a soft rule in code where anything with a complexity exceeding "7" (seven mentions in seven instances) should be refactored to decrease the likelihood of unnecessary code breaks when deploying your environment. Modularity in data engineering specifically refers to a design approach where the process is divided into separate, interchangeable components, each carrying out a specific function. This design ensures easier maintenance, enhanced readability, and greater reusability of code, which in turn enhances the scalability of the pipeline since this approach reduces the impact of future changes on the pipeline.

Auditing

Auditing is all about reinforcing data integrity and specific logging for compliance purposes. It's the intentional recording and reviewing of processes within the pipeline, such as data transformations and tracked errors, to provide transparency and accountability. In this way, organizations, both internal and external, can trust the accuracy and validity of data assets within the company. Data lineage tracking, change logs, and access controls can be easily monitored and tracked, so if/when an irregularity in the data does arise in the future, the auditing log can easily reveal if the irregularity was due to incorrect data management.

Summary

Designing a robust data pipeline is a forward-looking task. While we cannot predict all possible failures, we can certainly prepare for them by implementing sound architectural principles such as redundancy and fault tolerance. A robust ETL pipeline is not just about moving data from point A to point B efficiently; it's also about ensuring that the pipeline can recover from failures and ensure data integrity. Effective checkpointing and logging practices play a crucial role in this regard.

Logging serves as the eyes and ears of a data engineer. It provides real-time visibility into the operations of a pipeline, allowing for performance tracking and speedy troubleshooting of issues. The key to effective logging is to provide enough information to understand the what, when, and why of any event or error.

Modularity simplifies code maintenance, enhances readability, and allows for scalable design. It also facilitates code reuse—a module designed for a specific task can be utilized wherever that task is required, leading to a more consistent and efficient design.

Auditing is the process of recording and reviewing operations in a pipeline, capturing data transformations, and highlighting errors or exceptions. This component is essential for ensuring data accuracy, consistency, and compliance with regulations.

In summary, logging gives you insight into your pipeline's performance and potential issues. Modularity provides structure, promoting code reuse and easier maintenance. Auditing, finally, offers traceability and assists in ensuring data integrity and compliance. Together, these aspects form the bedrock of well-architected, efficient, and transparent data pipelines.

In our last chapter together, we will walk through some case studies of creating a robust data pipeline using the practices we have discussed throughout this book. We look forward to seeing you in the *Chapter 15*.

15

Use Cases and Further Reading

As we enter the last chapter of this book, we can look back on our path of understanding, designing, and building ETL pipelines in Python. We started by creating simple ETL pipelines in standard Python, then introduced ETL-specific Python modules to enhance our pipelines and create more efficient, reliable implementations. We introduced various external tools, including Apache Airflow and the AWS ecosystem, to expand your ETL foundation into the cloud. Finally, we brought ETL design full circle by discussing best practices regarding monitoring and logging your code, as well as common pitfalls to watch out for. We can confidently say that you now possess the foundational knowledge to deal with the diverse challenges of data extraction, transformation, and loading in today's data-driven world. However, to solidify and expand upon the concepts introduced in this book, you need to get comfortable with these workflows through repetitive practice.

In this chapter, we'll focus on the hands-on, practical, and development aspects of data pipelines. We will go through three application scenarios of operational deployments of ETL pipelines within real-world data analysis contexts. These exercises can then be used as a reference point and as sample data for you to test out the various ETL pipeline tools we have discussed throughout this book. This will demonstrate the power and efficiency of cloud-based ETL pipelines. Finally, we'll suggest further reading and resources to help you continue your learning journey in the ETL domain.

As we've just mentioned, this chapter and this book will conclude with a selection of recommended supplementary materials and resources. We highly encourage you to use these avenues for continued learning. Overall, we aim to reinforce the learning experience through hands-on exercises, which will provide you with a production-grade project that will boost your confidence in building ETL pipelines and jumpstart your career endeavors in data engineering.

This chapter will proceed as follows:

- Hands-on exercise for creating data pipelines
- Building a robust ETL pipeline with US construction data in AWS
- Further reading material

Technical requirements

To effectively utilize the resources and code examples provided in this chapter, ensure that your system meets the following technical requirements:

- Software requirements:

  - **Integrated development environment (IDE)**: We recommend using **PyCharm** as the preferred IDE for working with Python, and we might make specific references to PyCharm throughout this chapter. However, you are free to use any Python-compatible IDE of your choice.

  - Jupyter Notebooks should be installed.

  - Python version 3.6 or higher should be installed.

  - Pipenv should be installed for managing dependencies.

- GitHub repository:

  The associated code and resources for this chapter can be found in this book's GitHub repository at `https://github.com/PacktPublishing/Building-ETL-Pipelines-with-Python`. Fork and clone the repository to your local machine.

Hands-on exercise for creating data pipelines

Our first hands-on exercise aims to reinforce the design concepts and structures we've discussed throughout this book.

In this exercise, we will be working with an e-commerce dataset. The data consists of three CSV files: `orders.csv`, `products.csv`, and `customers.csv`. The `orders.csv` file contains details about each order, such as `order ID`, `customer ID`, `product ID`, `quantity`, and `order date`. The `products.csv` file contains information about each product, such as `product ID`, `name`, and `price`. Finally, the `customers.csv` file holds customer details, including `customer ID`, `name`, and `location`.

The goal of this exercise is to help you build an ETL pipeline that extracts data from these CSV files, performs several transformations (such as data cleaning, merging data, and calculating new metrics), and loads the results into a PostgreSQL database. The end product will be a refactored project directory in the following structure:

```
project: ecommerce
├── data
│   ├── orders.csv
│   ├── products.csv
│   └── customers.csv
├── etl
│   ├── __init__.py
```

```
|      ├── extract.py
|      ├── transform.py
|      └── load.py
└── config.yaml
└── pipeline.py
```

This example of e-commerce data is similar to working with legacy code in a work environment. Most of the time, legacy code was created under different conditions than the company's current situation, and coding practices were less stringent and probably less ideal as well. To diminish code debt within a company's code base, engineers are commonly asked to refactor and improve legacy code workflows.

The following code snippet represents a legacy ETL pipeline, which you'll be refactoring according to the structure outlined previously. We'll be refactoring the following code:

```python
# Import necessary libraries
import pandas as pd
from sqlalchemy import create_engine

# Step 1: Data Extraction
# Load the CSV files into pandas DataFrames
orders = pd.read_csv('orders.csv')
products = pd.read_csv('products.csv')
customers = pd.read_csv('customers.csv')

# Step 2: Data Transformation
# Clean data (e.g., handle missing values, correct data types)
orders = orders.dropna()
products = products.dropna()
customers = customers.dropna()

# Merge the orders and products DataFrames
data = pd.merge(orders, products, on='product_id')

# Calculate the total price for each order
data['total_price'] = data['quantity'] * data['price']
```

On the following page, we'll proceed with data merging and loading. Here is the code for merging and loading the data:

```python
# Merge the resulting DataFrame with the customers DataFrame
data = pd.merge(data, customers, on='customer_id')

# Step 3: Data Loading
# Create a connection to the PostgreSQL database
engine = create_engine('postgresql://username:password@localhost:5432/
```

```
mydatabase')

# Load the DataFrame into the database as a new table
data.to_sql('EcommerceData', engine, if_exists='replace', index=False)
```

Of course, if you head to the `chapter_15` GitHub directory, you'll find this already completed within the `e-commerce` project directory. However, for practice, start with the code in following sections and refactor each step, yourself, to create the preceding structure. You can download the necessary datasets from the GitHub repository for this chapter.

Through this exercise, you will get a chance to tackle challenges similar to those you would encounter in a real-world ETL scenario. For practice, try to refactor the preceding code using one to three of the ETL pipeline implementations we discussed in *Chapter 8*. Compare how each method performs, and which method feels the most comfortable for you to code with. This is all about repetition, building muscle memory, and having confidence in your ability to design data pipelines.

New York Yellow Taxi data, ETL pipeline, and deployment

The previous exercise was a great example of refactoring legacy, less ideal implementations of ETL pipelines into clean ETL design pipelines. However, the datasets we used were quite simple and not entirely reflective of data you will come across in reality. It also lacked the pillars of unit testing and validation, which inevitably diminished the potential robustness of the pipeline.

In this scenario, we'll take things a step further and build a pipeline that is more similar to what you might encounter in a professional setting. This pipeline will include professional coding practices, such as error handling, modularity for easy extension, and unit testing.

We will use New York 2021 Yellow Taxi Trip Data (`https://data.cityofnewyork.us/Transportation/2021-Yellow-Taxi-Trip-Data/m6nq-qud6`), an open source dataset that is significantly larger and more complex than the data in the previous example. It contains detailed information about taxi trips in New York City, such as pickup and drop-off times, trip distance, fare amount, and much more.

Using this structure, you will build a robust and production-grade ETL pipeline that extracts this data, performs three to five of the data transformation methods we discussed in *Chapter 5*, and loads the results into a PostgreSQL database. Once the pipeline is complete, you will need to add error handling and unit testing to strengthen your pipeline.

Step 1 – configuration

We'll start by setting up a configuration file. This file, named `config.py`, will contain all the configuration variables for the pipeline, such as the database connection string, the table name, and the file path. Storing these variables separately makes the code cleaner and easier to maintain:

```
# config.py
DATABASE_CONNECTION = 'postgresql://username:password@localhost:5432/
mydatabase'
TABLE_NAME = 'YellowTaxiData'
FILE_PATH = 'yellow_tripdata_2023-01.parquet'
```

Step 2 – ETL pipeline script

Next, we'll create the main script for the ETL pipeline. This script, `etl_pipeline.py`, will include functions for each step of the ETL process: `extract_data()`, `transform_data()`, and `load_data()`. Each function will be equipped with error handling to manage potential issues that might occur during the execution of the pipeline:

```
# etl_pipeline.py
import pandas as pd
from sqlalchemy import create_engine
from config import DATABASE_CONNECTION, TABLE_NAME, FILE_PATH

def extract_data(file_path):
    # < code here >
    return df

def transform_data(df):
    # < code here >
    return df

def load_data(df, table_name, database_connection):
            engine = create_engine(redshift_conn_str)
            df.to_sql(table_name, engine,
            if_exists = 'replace',index=False)
def run_etl_pipeline():
    df = extract_data(FILE_PATH)
    df = transform_data(df)
    load_data(df, TABLE_NAME, DATABASE_CONNECTION)
```

Step 3 – unit tests

Lastly, we must ensure the reliability of our pipeline by writing unit tests. These tests will verify the correctness of each function in the pipeline and will help us catch any issues or regressions as we continue to modify and extend our code.

In this section, we will provide one to three unit tests that can be performed on each of the ETL activities. However, please feel free to add as many as you see fit; the more unit tests you have, the more robust your data pipeline:

```
# test_etl_pipeline.py
import unittest
from etl_pipeline import extract_data, transform_data, load_data
from config import DATABASE_CONNECTION, TABLE_NAME, FILE_PATH


class TestETLPipeline(unittest.TestCase):
```

We utilize `unittest.TestCase` as the input value for the `TestETLPipeline()` class to create test assertions for key aspects of each ETL step.

First, we need to assert that the DataFrame created by the `extract_data ()` function is not empty (`self.assertIsNotNone(df)`) and has 18 columns (`self.assertEqual(df.shape[1], 18)`):

```
    def test_extract_data(self):
        df = extract_data(FILE_PATH)
        self.assertIsNotNone(df)
        self.assertEqual(df.shape[1], 18)
```

Next, we must assert that the DataFrame that was created by the `transform_data ()` function contains the `trip_duration` column (`self.assertIn('trip_duration', df.columns)`) and the `average_speed` column (`self.assertIn('average_speed', df.columns)`):

```
    def test_transform_data(self):
        df = extract_data(FILE_PATH)
        df = transform_data(df)
        self.assertIn('trip_duration', df.columns)
        self.assertIn('average_speed', df.columns)
```

Finally, we must assert that the connection to the PostgreSQL output data location of the `load()` function works and that the resulting schema of the data table is the same structure that's required. We can accomplish this by performing two tests:

```
    def test_load_data(self):
        df = extract_data(FILE_PATH)
        df = transform_data(df)
```

```
            load_data(df, TABLE_NAME, DATABASE_CONNECTION)
        # In a standard use case, it is common to establish a database
    connection and perform validation
    if __name__ == '__main__':
        unittest.main()
```

This exercise provides a framework and workflow for how to develop ETL pipelines that are suitable for deployment in real-world professional scenarios. By working with this large and complex dataset, you'll gain a better understanding of the challenges and intricacies of building robust ETL pipelines, most notably how larger datasets emphasize the importance of writing optimized, maintainable code that is scanned for correctness through testing.

As practice, try to refactor the preceding code using some of the AWS tools we discussed in *Chapters 9 to 11* since using cloud services adds scalability to your data pipelines. Play around with the AWS resources and get comfortable with at least one cloud implementation of your data pipeline.

Building a robust ETL pipeline with US construction data in AWS

In this section, we'll dive into a real-world scenario by constructing an ETL pipeline using US construction market data, which is conveniently available through the AWS Marketplace: `https://aws.amazon.com/marketplace/pp/prodview-6dxonc3cvfpeq#dataSets`. The **Construction Marketing Data Warehouse (CMDW)** contains an array of residential, commercial, and solar construction projects, as well as businesses operating within the US. This gives you a lot of content to play around with! As with the previous sections of this chapter, we will initiate a simplistic approach to developing an AWS data pipeline for the CMDW data; we highly encourage you to spend some time building out this pipeline to a professional level.

Prerequisites

This pipeline will write data to and from an AWS S3 bucket. As you may recall from *Chapter 10*, we must use the `boto3` Python module to connect to S3. We've listed `boto3` and the other required libraries in a `requirements.txt` file for easy installation:

```
boto3==1.18.33
pandas==1.3.2
sqlalchemy==1.4.22
```

You can install these libraries using `pip` by running the following command in your Python environment:

```
pipenv install -r requirements.txt
```

Step 1 – data extraction

We'll start with importing the library:

```
import boto3
```

To extract the US Construction data from AWS, we will use a combination of `boto3` and the AWS SDK for Python to download the US construction market data from an S3 bucket on AWS:

```
def extract_data(bucket_name, file_key, local_path):
    s3 = boto3.client('s3')
    s3.download_file(bucket_name, file_key, local_path)s
    print(f"Downloaded {file_key} from {bucket_name} to {local_
path}")
```

Step 2 – data transformation

Let's assume that we're interested in the duration of the projects. Our dataset includes columns for the start and end dates of each construction project. We can use the `pandas` library in Python to perform these transformations:

```
import pandas as pd

def transform_data(local_path):
    df = pd.read_csv(local_path)
    df['start_date'] = pd.to_datetime(df['start_date'])
    df['end_date'] = pd.to_datetime(df['end_date'])
    df['duration'] = df['end_date'] - df['start_date']
    df.loc[df['end_date'].isna(),
    'duration'] = pd.Timestamp.today() - df['start_date']
    df['duration'] = df['duration'].dt.days
    print(f"Transformed data from {local_path}")
    return df
```

Step 3 – data loading

The final location for the US Construction data will be an Amazon Redshift cluster. We can use the `sqlalchemy` Python module to load the data into Redshift:

```
from sqlalchemy import create_engine

def load_data(df, table_name, redshift_conn_str):
    engine = create_engine(redshift_conn_str)
    df.to_sql(table_name, engine, if_exists='replace',
```

```
        index=False)
        print(f"Loaded data into {table_name}")
```

Running the ETL pipeline

In your code file, create the following parameters based on how you set up your AWS S3 environment:

```
# Lazy - Import of Paths
# TODO: Create config.yaml file
s3_BUCKET_NAME = "your_s3_bucket_name"
CMDW_FILE_KEY = "your_filename"
LOCAL_PATH = "data/us_construction_extract.csv"
REDSHIFT_TABLE = "your_redshift_table"
REDSHIFT_CONN_STR = "your_redshift_conn_str"
```

Now, we can create a simple function to run the entire ETL pipeline:

```
def run_etl_pipeline(bucket_name, file_key, local_path, table_name,
redshift_conn_str):
        extract_data(bucket_name, file_key, local_path)
        df = transform_data(local_path)
        load_data(df, table_name, redshift_conn_str)
```

Finally, we can make the script deployable as a Python script:

```
if __name__ == '__main__':
    run_etl_pipeline(bucket_name=s3_BUCKET_NAME,
                            file_key=CMDW_FILE_KEY,
                            local_path=LOCAL_PATH,
                            table_name=REDSHIFT_TABLE,
                            redshift_conn_str=REDSHIFT_CONN_STR)
```

Bonus – deploying your ETL pipeline

As we've learned throughout this book, the deployment process of an ETL pipeline is where the pipeline environment is configured to run automatically, either on a regular schedule or in response to a trigger.

We will give you the general steps on how to deploy your pipeline with AWS, but we won't do the heavy lifting for you in this chapter! Feel free to comb through *Parts 3 and 4* for any reminders or improved methodologies to run your pipeline on so that it can automatically scale to handle large amounts of data.

Now, it's your turn to explore these details further. Here are some general steps on how to deploy your pipeline in AWS:

1. Set up an AWS account and configure the necessary services.

2. Modify your ETL script so that it runs in the cloud environment. *Pro tip: Move your pipeline to a bucket on AWS S3.*

3. Set up a schedule or trigger for your pipeline in the AWS console.

Due to the complexity of these steps and the variety of ways to deploy an ETL pipeline, we won't go into more detail here. However, we encourage you to use one to three AWS workflows to deploy your data pipeline automatically, in batch, and whatever use case of deployment suits your curiosity. If you need more guidance, head back to *Chapters 9 to 12* for some quick reviews, or check out AWS' extensive documentation and tutorials.

Summary

Congratulations on reaching the end of this book! You've worked hard and learned about ETL pipelines and how to build them from scratch with Python. You also gained hands-on experience dealing with real-world data and constructing ETL pipelines in an enterprise environment using AWS.

We encourage you to explore and play with data. Come up with innovative requirements and solve them. This is a great way to learn and grow in the field. Remember, the key to mastering the development of robust data pipelines is practice. So, don't hesitate to get your hands dirty with the data. Happy coding!

Further reading

The field of data engineering is vast and constantly evolving. There's always more to learn and explore. Always prioritize staying up-to-date with the latest developments and best practices in the field.

Here are some recommended resources for further continued learning:

*   *AWS Big Data Blog* (`https://aws.amazon.com/blogs/big-data/`): This blog provides a wealth of information on various topics related to big data on AWS, including ETL processes, data warehousing, and analytics.

*   *Python for Data Analysis*, by Wes McKinney (`https://www.amazon.com/Python-Data-Analysis-Wrangling-IPython/dp/1491957662?_encoding=UTF8&tag=embracingaugmentation-20&linkCode=ur2&linkId=7b622b5207f4c59b89834da4633457b5&camp=1789&creative=9325`): This book is a comprehensive guide to using Python for data analysis. It covers various topics, including data cleaning, transformation, and visualization.

- *Streaming Systems*, by Tyler Akidau, Slava Chernyak, and Reuven Lax (`https://www.amazon.com/Streaming-Systems-Where-Large-Scale-Processing/dp/1491983876/`): This book explores the what, where, when, and how of data processing, diving into the data layer that powers both batch and streaming data processing.

- *Designing Data-Intensive Applications*, by Martin Kleppmann (`https://www.amazon.com/Designing-Data-Intensive-Applications-Reliable-Maintainable/dp/B08VL1BLHB`): This book provides a broad understanding of databases and distributed systems for data scalability and consistency.

- *Apache Kafka* (`https://kafka.apache.org/`): Apache Kafka is a distributed streaming platform that can be used to build real-time data pipelines. Their website provides a wealth of information and tutorials to get you started.

- *Data Engineering on Google Cloud Professional Certificate* (`https://www.coursera.org/professional-certificates/gcp-data-engineering`): This online course on Coursera is designed to provide a hands-on introduction to designing and building data processing systems on Google Cloud.

- *ETL with Apache Airflow* (`https://airflow.apache.org/docs/apache-airflow/stable/tutorial/fundamentals.html`): Apache Airflow is an open source platform that's designed to programmatically author, schedule, and monitor workflows. The Airflow documentation and community are an excellent resource for those interested in ETL processes.

Index

www.packtpub.com

Subscribe to our online digital library for full access to over 7,000 books and videos, as well as industry leading tools to help you plan your personal development and advance your career. For more information, please visit our website.

Why subscribe?

- Spend less time learning and more time coding with practical eBooks and Videos from over 4,000 industry professionals

- Improve your learning with Skill Plans built especially for you

- Get a free eBook or video every month

- Fully searchable for easy access to vital information

- Copy and paste, print, and bookmark content

Did you know that Packt offers eBook versions of every book published, with PDF and ePub files available? You can upgrade to the eBook version at packtpub.com and as a print book customer, you are entitled to a discount on the eBook copy. Get in touch with us at customercare@packtpub.com for more details.

At www.packtpub.com, you can also read a collection of free technical articles, sign up for a range of free newsletters, and receive exclusive discounts and offers on Packt books and eBooks.

Other Books You May Enjoy

If you enjoyed this book, you may be interested in these other books by Packt:

Data Engineering with Python

Paul Crickard

ISBN: 978-1-83921-418-9

- Understand how data engineering supports data science workflows
- Discover how to extract data from files and databases and then clean, transform, and enrich it
- Configure processors for handling different file formats as well as both relational and
- NoSQL databases
- Find out how to implement a data pipeline and dashboard to visualize results
- Use staging and validation to check data before landing in the warehouse
- Build real-time pipelines with staging areas that perform validation and handle failures
- Get to grips with deploying pipelines in the production environment

Serverless ETL and Analytics with AWS Glue

Vishal Pathak, Subramanya Vajiraya, Noritaka Sekiyama, Tomohiro Tanaka, Albert Quiroga, Ishan Gaur

ISBN: 978-1-80056-498-5

- Apply various AWS Glue features to manage and create data lakes
- Use Glue DataBrew and Glue Studio for data preparation
- Optimize data layout in cloud storage to accelerate analytics workloads
- Manage metadata including database, table, and schema definitions
- Secure your data during access control, encryption, auditing, and networking
- Monitor AWS Glue jobs to detect delays and loss of data
- Integrate Spark ML and SageMaker with AWS Glue to create machine learning models

Packt is searching for authors like you

If you're interested in becoming an author for Packt, please visit authors.packtpub.com and apply today. We have worked with thousands of developers and tech professionals, just like you, to help them share their insight with the global tech community. You can make a general application, apply for a specific hot topic that we are recruiting an author for, or submit your own idea.

Share Your Thoughts

Now you've finished *Building ETL Pipelines with Python*, we'd love to hear your thoughts! Scan the QR code below to go straight to the Amazon review page for this book and share your feedback or leave a review on the site that you purchased it from.

https://packt.link/r/1-804-61525-0

Your review is important to us and the tech community and will help us make sure we're delivering excellent quality content.

Download a free PDF copy of this book

Thanks for purchasing this book!

Do you like to read on the go but are unable to carry your print books everywhere?

Is your eBook purchase not compatible with the device of your choice?

Don't worry, now with every Packt book you get a DRM-free PDF version of that book at no cost.

Read anywhere, any place, on any device. Search, copy, and paste code from your favorite technical books directly into your application.

The perks don't stop there, you can get exclusive access to discounts, newsletters, and great free content in your inbox daily

Follow these simple steps to get the benefits:

1. Scan the QR code or visit the link below

https://packt.link/free-ebook/978-1-80461-525-6

2. Submit your proof of purchase
3. That's it! We'll send your free PDF and other benefits to your email directly